the COMMANDMENTS *we* KEEP

They are timeless and timely, these Ten Commandments, and Msgr. Peter Vaghi combines the realism of a pastor with the precision of a theologian to "bring them down the mountain" for us today.

Most Reverend Timothy M. Dolan
Archbishop of New York
President of the United States Conference of Catholic Bishops

Msgr. Peter Vaghi offers a fresh and engaging look at the Decalogue. He addresses the moral teaching of the Church with the skill of a good teacher and the understanding of a caring pastor.

Cardinal Donald W. Wuerl
Archbishop of Washington

In a culture permeated with moral relativism and egoism, Msgr. Vaghi has provided a timely and effective antidote. His thoughtful, lucid and insightful explanation of the Ten Commandments helps us to understand the moral life as Christ intends and live it with Christian hope and true fulfillment.

Most Reverend Paul S. Loverde
Bishop of Arlington

"Living differently" and "living an examined life" are the challenges that unite Msgr. Peter J. Vaghi's vibrant exposition of the Ten Commandments in this timely book. Priests, adult educators, and catechists will find here a positive, well researched, and eloquently expressed presentation of Catholic Christian morality. The author has done a superb job of synthesizing the Old and New Testament background of each commandment, recent Church teaching, and traditional principles of moral theology.

Msgr. Francis D. Kelly
Author of *Through the Church Year*

An engaging and comprehensive presentation of what it means to live a Catholic moral life. The questions and prayers help to prayerfully deepen the understanding of the law of God. A great resource for catechetical leaders and catechists.

Maruja Sedano
Director
Office for Catechesis and Youth Ministry
Archdiocese of Chicago

the
COMMANDMENTS
we
KEEP

A Catholic Guide
to Living a Moral Life

PETER J.
VAGHI

foreword by
Archbishop Edwin F. O'Brien

ave maria press AmP notre dame, indiana

Nihil Obstat: Monsignor Michael Heintz, PhD
                  Censor Librorum

Imprimatur: Most Reverend Kevin C. Rhoades
                  Bishop of Fort Wayne–South Bend

Given at Fort Wayne, Indiana on October 23, 2010

Founded in 1865, Ave Maria Press is a ministry of the Indiana Province of Holy Cross.

www.avemariapress.com

ISBN-10 1-59471-261-1 ISBN-13 978-1-59471-261-6

Cover image © Superstock/Photononstop
Cover design by David Scholtes and Katherine Ross.
Text design by David Scholtes.
Printed and bound in the United States of America.

Library of Congress Cataloging-in-Publication Data
Vaghi, Peter J.
  The commandments we keep : a Catholic guide to living a moral life / Peter J. Vaghi.
      p. cm.
  Includes bibliographical references (pp. 141-144).
  ISBN-13: 978-1-59471-261-6 (pbk.)
  ISBN-10: 1-59471-261-1 (pbk.)
  1. Ten commandments. 2. Christian ethics--Catholic authors. I. Title.
  BV4655.V24 2011
  241'.042--dc22

                                    2010047149

Dedicated to David P. Durbin, exemplary husband and father, outstanding lawyer, twenty-eighth President of the John Carroll Society, and dear friend. He taught us how to live and he taught us how to die. May he rest in peace! (1948–2010)

Special gratitude to the parishioners of Little Flower Parish and members of the John Carroll Society; to my editor, Robert Hamma; to Gerald O'Collins, S.J.; Father Christopher Begg; Adoreen McCormick; Gregory J. Granitto; and Kevin McIntyre.

The Pillars of Faith Series
by Peter J. Vaghi

*The Faith We Profess: A Catholic Guide to the Apostles'
Creed*
*The Sacraments We Celebrate: A Catholic Guide to the
Seven Mysteries of Faith*
*The Commandments We Keep: A Catholic Guide to Living a
Moral Life*

.

CONTENTS

Foreword

In this, the third of four pastoral commentaries on the *Catechism of the Catholic Church*, Monsignor Peter J. Vaghi brings insights gleaned from many years as pastor and lover of theology to the third pillar of the Catechism, "Life in Christ." Those familiar with his prior books on the first two pillars, *The Faith We Profess* and *The Sacraments We Celebrate*, will find in this volume a perceptive eye on the Catechism's teachings and the life of everyday Catholics in a culture where "it can't be so wrong if it feels so right."

The two great commandments—love of God and love of neighbor—are fleshed out by the author's treatment of each of the Ten Commandments: first, through a very helpful Introduction, and then by demonstrating each of the precepts as ordinances of love in themselves and foundational to the understanding of Christ's teaching in the Sermon on the Mount.

Readers might be unaware of Monsignor Vaghi's background and apostolic endeavors: his prior life as a well respected lawyer who continues to offer Catholic counsel to that profession and whose generous availability has prompted a good number of notables—and not so notables—to embrace our faith; as chaplain of the John Carroll Society, seeking to engage Catholic professionals in a serious examination and living out of this faith; and, most especially, as pastor of the historic parish of St. Patrick in Washington and now of the Church of the Little Flower in Bethesda, Maryland. Each step along the way, his profound Catholic faith and love of our Catholic Church have had an enormous impact upon the faith of the capital city and far beyond. Solid credentials such as these cast light on the reason for the clarity and persuasiveness of *The Commandments We Keep*.

I unreservedly recommend this book as a valuable resource in adult faith formation, especially in RCIA. It represents a distinctive style of catechesis, incorporating Sacred Scripture, the "new" Catechism (while not abandoning the Baltimore Catechism!), and the teachings of the most recent extraordinary pontiffs, Pope John Paul II and Pope Benedict XVI. Pew-filling Catholics—and there might well be more of them if this volume is used seriously—will rejoice in seeing their faith deeply rooted in the Ten Commandments. And what ecumenical and inter-faith possibilities this offers to parish discussion groups, councils, and committees in relating the truths of our rich faith—not only to our Protestant friends but also to our senior brothers and sisters in faith of the Jewish tradition. For Catholics, *The Commandments We Keep* is an invitation not only to study our faith and come to a deeper understanding of it, but to pray, to share our faith with others, and to give witness to the Gospel of Our Lord, Jesus Christ.

There is one more book to follow in this series—on prayer. I must thank Monsignor Vaghi for his continuing effort—among his very many responsibilities and ministries in his parish and archdiocese—to explain our faith to new and distant audiences in this ever changing culture in which we Catholics are privileged to live our faith.

Most Reverend Edwin F. O'Brien
Archbishop of Baltimore

Preface

One of the most persistent questions in life, one that sums up our efforts to define our relationship with one another and with God, is "How shall I live?" In response to this perennial human inquiry, a host of answers have been proposed. Often an appeal is made to public opinion polls. Yet we, as followers of Christ, know that the norm for moral conduct is found in God's law. Morality is another word for living a good, full, decent life according to right choices.

When asked "What good must I do to gain eternal life?" Jesus' response was clear, concise, and direct: "If you wish to enter into life, keep the commandments" (Mt 19:17).

Monsignor Peter Vaghi here offers a fresh and engaging look at the Decalogue. He addresses the moral teaching of the Church with the skill of a good teacher and the understanding of a caring pastor. To anyone who wants to know the meaning of the Ten Commandments for their lives today, he provides wise guidance for fruitful thought, reflection, and prayer. He does so with the eyes of a pastor who understands how a deeper study of the commandments helps us in our lifelong journey to form our consciences and to live in spiritual freedom. Monsignor Vaghi's book is recommended for those who seek both the challenge and inspiration to walk in the light of the Commandments.

Donald Cardinal Wuerl
Archbishop of Washington

Introduction

This is the third book in a series that looks at the four pillars of the *Catechism of the Catholic Church*: The Profession of Faith, The Celebration of the Christian Mystery, Life in Christ, and Christian Prayer. The first book, *The Faith We Profess: A Catholic Guide to the Apostles' Creed*, examined the twelve articles of the Apostles' Creed. The second book, *The Sacraments We Celebrate: A Catholic Guide to the Seven Mysteries of Faith*, focused on the seven sacraments as transforming encounters with Christ. In this third volume, we reflect on the moral teaching of the Church with emphasis on the Ten Commandments.

What do we hope that these nine chapters on the moral life, and the commandments in particular, will accomplish? There are four hopes.

1. To come to know the commandments and their implications for us

Since most of us learned the Ten Commandments (often called the Decalogue) when we were children, the tendency may be for us to remember them simply through the eyes and ears of children. Normally we think of two tablets. The first three commandments, which concern love of God, appear on one tablet; and on the second are written the seven commandments that involve love of neighbor. The biblical basis of the Ten Commandments is found in two places in the Old Testament: Exodus 20 and Deuteronomy 5. The Deuteronomy passage is generally thought to be the later text where Moses recalls events that took place forty years previously. Hopefully, this book will help us understand the commandments in a new and mature way and see more clearly their wide implications for our lives as followers of Jesus Christ.

2. To understand that the Ten Commandments, given to the Israelites on Mount Sinai, are not abolished for those of us who are followers of Jesus Christ

Quite the contrary, as Christians, we are empowered to live the Ten Commandments in a new way. We are invited to rediscover the law in the person of Jesus Christ, who is the perfect fulfillment of the law. "Do not think that I have come to abolish the law or the prophets. I have come not to abolish but to fulfill" (Mt 5:17). It will become clear that Jesus, while underscoring love as the principal commandment, built upon and expanded what Moses was given on Mount Sinai.

The preacher of the papal household, Father Raniero Cantalamessa, in his book, *Life in Christ*, writes perceptively: "St. John says that 'the law was given through Moses, but grace and truth came through Jesus Christ.' If we apply this today to ourselves in the Church, it means that man can make the law and founders can make rules of life, but only Jesus Christ, with his Spirit, can give the strength to live them."

Our late Holy Father, John Paul II, on February 26, 2000, at St. Catherine's Monastery at the foot of Mount Sinai said:

> The Ten Commandments are not an arbitrary imposition of a tyrannical Lord. They

were written in stone; but before that, they were written on the human heart as the universal moral law, valid in every time and place. Today as always, the Ten Words of the law provide the only true basis for the lives of individuals, societies and nations. Today as always, they are the only future of the human family. They save man from the destructive force of egoism, hatred and falsehood. They point out all the false gods that draw him into slavery: the love of self to the exclusion of God, the greed for power and pleasure that overturns the order of justice and degrades our human dignity and that of our neighbor. If we turn from these false idols and follow the God who sets his people free and remains always with them, then we shall emerge like Moses, after forty days on the mountain, "shining with glory" (Saint Gregory of Nyssa, *The Life of Moses,* II, 230), ablaze with the light of God!

To keep the Commandments is to be faithful to God, but it is also to be faithful to ourselves, to our true nature and our deepest aspirations.

The figure of Christ glorified on Mount Tabor in his Transfiguration reminds us that only in Christ, who died and rose for us, is it possible that the commandments, given on Mount Sinai, can be lived in a new way. This is what it means that Tabor fulfills Sinai. This is what is new about the Good News of the Gospel, which Jesus came to give us. This is a word of great hope for us who are called to live the commandments as the basis of our lives and as our hope for eternal life.

3. To see that we come to know Christ precisely in our efforts to keep the commandments

> The way we may be sure that we know him is to keep his commandments. Whoever says, "I know him," but does not keep his commandments is a liar, and the truth is not in him. But whoever keeps his word, the love of God is truly perfected in him. This is the way we may know that we are in union with him; whoever claims to abide in him ought to live [just] as he lived. (1 Jn 2:3–6)

We come to know God when we seek to follow the commandments. In other words, it is the actual attempt to live the commandments, in doing what we are asked to do with God's help, that we come into relationship with God. It is then that we come to know and love him. This profound awareness has had an incredible effect on my spiritual journey. I hope you will experience the same realization—that it is precisely in our effort to follow the commandments that we come in contact with the living God and his deep and abiding love for us. "If you keep my commandments, you will remain in my love, just as I have kept my Father's commandments and remain in his love" (Jn 15:10).

4. To use the commandments as a basis for our daily examination of conscience

Hopefully, a deepened study of the commandments will help us in the ongoing challenge to form our consciences and give us a deeper spiritual freedom that results from confessing our sins regularly and living the love commands of our Lord. In the Appendix of this book, there is a guide to confession and an examination of conscience.

In addition, after each chapter, there are reflection questions and a prayer. These resources enable a small group to gather to reflect together on their faith. The prayer provided, or any familiar prayer, hymn, or psalm can be used to open and/or conclude each gathering. Of course, these resources can also be used personally to reflect and pray as one proceeds through this process.

The nine chapters will draw from the great tradition of our Catholic faith as expressed in the universal *Catechism of the Catholic Church (CCC)* and the *United States Catholic Catechism for Adults (USCCA)*. We will also examine the moral life through the prism of the writings of our late Holy Father John Paul II and of Pope Benedict XVI. References in the text to the *Catechism of the Catholic Church* are accompanied by the paragraph number, for example (*CCC* 572). References to the *United States Catholic Catechism for Adults* are given by the page number, for example (*USCCA* 165). Throughout the book you will also find references to the writings of John Paul II, Benedict XVI, other popes, theologians, and writers, as well as the documents of the Second Vatican Council. These documents are referred to by their English names, often accompanied by their corresponding Latin titles, and referenced by the Latin titles' abbreviations. For example, Pope Benedict XVI's encyclical, *Saved by Hope*, is referenced as *SS* for its Latin title, *Spe Salvi*, followed by the paragraph number. (Abbreviations are listed at the end of the book.) With the exception of the documents of the Second Vatican Council, which are quoted from the edition edited by Austin Flannery, all other Church documents quoted in this book are taken from the Vatican website: www.vatican.va. The site has an excellent search engine. For the most efficient search results, enter the Latin name of the document. When quotations are taken from addresses by the Holy Father, these are noted by date. The full text of these addresses can be found by searching the Vatican website by date. Other sources quoted are referenced at the end of the book. These citations are arranged by chapter in the order in which they appear.

ONE

The One Who Has Faith Lives Differently

The title of this first chapter is adapted from Pope Benedict's second encyclical, *Saved by Hope*, in which the Holy Father writes: "The one who has hope lives differently." The use of the word *faith* captures the essence of this entire book, that the faith must be lived in a hopeful way. At its heart, moreover, living the faith is about free choices. We make choices each day: at home with our families, in the workplace, at places of recreation, and during the time we spend alone. Understood properly, "human freedom is more than a capacity to choose between this and that. It is the God-given power to become who he created us to be and so to share eternal union with him" (*USCCA* 310). To live in this way is the basis of our hope as followers of Jesus. Understood in this way, true freedom makes it possible for us to live differently than the popular understanding of freedom that is defined by simply doing what *I* wish to do.

How then does our Catholic faith—a faith rooted in the living person of Jesus Christ—give us direction and inner strength to make the right choices? How is it that our faith helps us form our consciences to make those correct choices? At the outset, we must define what conscience is. Simply stated by the Second Vatican Council, "conscience is man's most secret core, and his sanctuary. There he is alone with God whose voice echoes in his depths" (GS 16). The Council also teaches that the "voice, ever calling him to love and to do what is good and to avoid evil, tells him inwardly at the right moment: do this, shun that" (GS 16). Following one's conscience has consequences. Carl A. Anderson points to the beloved English saint, Thomas More, as an appropriate guide: "For he used all his brilliance as a lawyer to avoid conflict with King Henry VIII. Yet, finally, when direct conflict could no longer be avoided, he sacrificed both his family's security and his very life for the sake of his Catholic conscience." In that same article, Anderson quotes the then–Cardinal Ratzinger's reference to the conversion to Catholicism of Blessed John Henry Newman. Cardinal Ratzinger stated that Newman's "conversion to Catholicism cost him dearly and came about as a need to obey the truth in his conscience. In a letter to the Duke of Norfolk, Newman wrote, 'If I am obliged to bring religion into after-dinner toasts . . . I shall drink—to the Pope, if you please—still, to Conscience first, and to the Pope afterwards.'"

Both More and Newman had clearly formed consciences. Conscience formation is a lifelong effort, and it takes place according to objective moral standards. "The Word of God is a principal tool in the formation of conscience when it is assimilated by study, prayer, and practice" (USCCA 314). In addition, our consciences are formed with the prudent advice and good example of others, especially the authoritative teaching of the Church and the gifts of the Holy Spirit. Traditionally, the work of conscience formation has taken place in parishes, Catholic schools and, above all, in the family.

For this reason, the strengthening of family life is a most important priority in the New Evangelization.

As described by Pope Benedict, the New Evangelization is:

> . . . a renewed evangelization in the countries where the first proclamation of the faith has already resonated and where Churches with an ancient foundation exist but are experiencing the progressive secularization of society and a sort of "eclipse of the sense of God," which pose a challenge to finding appropriate means to propose anew the perennial truth of Christ's Gospel. (June 28, 2010)

Or as Washington Cardinal Donald Wuerl writes in his pastoral letter on the New Evangelization:

> Somehow in what we do and how we express our faith, we have to be able to repropose our belief in Christ and his Gospel for a hearing among those who are convinced that they already know the faith and it holds no interest for them. We have to invite them to hear it all over again, this time for the first time.

The New Evangelization is ultimately about a new and hopeful way of looking at the world and living in it through the lens of a welcoming Gospel. In his magnificent encyclical, *Saved by Hope (Spe Salvi)*, Benedict XVI teaches us: "The one who has hope lives differently: the one who hopes has been granted the gift of a new life"

(*SS* 2). At its heart, then, the moral life is about living that informed hope within us. But how is this possible?

The answer can be found in Galatians 2:20, where St. Paul writes, "Yet I live, no longer I, but Christ lives in me." These are revolutionary words. Do we ever stop to think about their impact? Christ lives within us. His presence, to the extent we yield to it and to the presence of his Holy Spirit, makes us live different and more hopeful lives. We are not alone. Not only are we made in the image and likeness of God, which is a basic principle of the moral life and our human dignity; but by his living presence within us, we are able to act differently and live more hopefully. He so desires to express himself through our facial expressions, the tone of our voices, even our body language. You and I are credible witnesses to our faith to the extent that we mirror the living presence of Christ within us. This is my daily challenge as a priest and the challenge for each of us in our very hectic and busy lives at home and in our workplaces.

Along with Pope Benedict, we must ask ourselves daily whether our Christian faith is "'performative' for us—is it a message which shapes our life in a new way, or is it just 'information' which, in the meantime, we have set aside and which now seems to us to have been superseded by more recent information" (*SS* 10)? In that same encyclical, *Saved by Hope*, the Pope answers beautifully:

> Christianity was not only "good news"—the communication of a hitherto unknown content. In our language we would say: the Christian message was not only "informative" but "performative." That means:

the Gospel is not merely a communication of things that can be known—it is one that makes things happen and is life-changing. (*SS* 2)

But how?

It happens through daily encounters with the living God within us. Our challenge is to be in regular communication, regular touch with him in our prayer, in our study, in our sacramental encounters, in our concern and love for the poor, in our sacrifices for one another, in our living as Jesus lived and continues to live. It is another name for grace—that life in Christ and the inner presence of the Holy Spirit. "The grace that comes to us from Christ in the Spirit is as essential as love and rules and, in fact, makes love and keeping the rules possible" (*USCCA* 318). In effect, that is the moral life: the faith lived, the subject of this book.

Jesus Christ is the ultimate teacher of the moral life. He ratified the Ten Commandments, adopted them as his own, deepened them, and showed us how each is an example of the love of God or the love of neighbor. Together, they are fundamental to the moral life. Speaking of the Ten Commandments as the love of God and neighbor and their relationship to Christ, Pope Benedict said in a homily on Palm Sunday, 2010, that "the Ten Commandments read in a new and deeper way beginning with Christ are part of this love. These commandments are nothing other than the basic rules of true love" (March 28, 2010). In addition, the Beatitudes are taught by Jesus, and they "give spirit to the law of the Ten Commandments and bring perfection to the moral life" (*USCCA* 309).

All three of the synoptic gospels (Matthew, Mark, and Luke) contain the story of the rich young man. It is the same text used in that Magna-Carta encyclical on the moral life, *The Splendor of Truth (Veritatis Splendor)*. It is also used in the *United States Catholic Catechism for Adults* at the beginning of Part III, "Christian Morality: The Faith Lived" (*USCCA* 307).

In Matthew 19:16–22 we read that "someone approached" Jesus and asked him a question. We have no idea who that someone is. No name is given, although we learn later in the text that it is a young man. It is probably just as well that we do not know initially who it is. It could be you or I. So put yourself in that scene right now. Try and ask Jesus the same question: "Teacher, what good must I do to gain eternal life?" Is this even the kind of question you would raise today? When was the last time you thought about eternal life? Most of us are focused, perhaps unduly, on the pressing demands of the here and now with our iPhones and BlackBerrys, voice mails and faxes. Various habits of successful time management have been ingrained in us.

How does Jesus answer the question? He says directly: "There is only One who is good. If you wish to enter into life, keep the commandments." He does not list rules and regulations, at least initially. No, he speaks of the good. "The good is belonging to God, obeying him, walking humbly with him in doing justice and in loving kindness" (*VS* 11).

Almost immediately, Jesus tells the young man to keep the commandments. As if to appropriate the Jewish law, Jesus summarizes the commandments and makes them his own: "You shall not murder; you shall not commit adultery; you shall not bear false witness;

honor your father and your mother; also, you shall love your neighbor as yourself" (*VS* 13). When the rich young man told Jesus he had done all of that, Jesus told him to live the love command in its most radical form—go sell what you have and give to the poor. The commandments "are the *first necessary step on the journey towards freedom*, its starting point " (*VS* 13). Only then did Jesus say: "Come, follow me."

I learned a most significant lesson from *The Splendor of Truth*, the same lesson that Jesus was trying to teach the rich young man. The moral life for a Christian is not simply about rules and regulations, as important and indeed essential as the Ten Commandments are. Fundamentally, the moral life is about life in Christ Jesus, about following him and living in him. This is made possible first of all because of our Baptism into him and by all the graces that flow from him—from the sacraments, from our prayer, and from our lives of service. No mere human effort alone succeeds in our fulfilling the law, no matter how hard we try. "This fulfillment can come only from a gift of God: the offer of a share in the divine Goodness revealed and communicated in Jesus. . . . What the young man now perhaps only dimly perceives will in the end be fully revealed by Jesus himself in the invitation: 'Come, follow me'" (*VS* 11).

The Ten Commandments give us guidance and make it possible for us to know the truth as he gives the truth to us. And Jesus teaches us that "the truth will set you free" (Jn 8:32). In his very person, Jesus *is* the Splendor of Truth. And Jesus came not to destroy the law, the law of Moses, but to fulfill it. He fulfilled the law precisely in and through his very person. In his dying, rising, and sending the Holy Spirit, he sends his life and his love to us. He pours his love in us by the power of the Holy Spirit that enables us to live as he teaches us.

The Christian life is thus about a love affair with the person Jesus. The rules and regulations of that relationship are a part of a covenant first given to the Israelites in the Ten Commandments (or Decalogue) on Mount Sinai. It was a covenant relationship, which set them free from their oppressors and gave them a new way of living. All the more did Christ give you and me a new way of living and loving in and through him and our daily relationship with him. In Baptism, you and I were freed from the slavery and inheritance of sin and made sharers in his life, a life destined for life eternal, a life of hope.

In his homily preached in Rome on June 11, 2010, at the closing of the Year for Priests, Pope Benedict succinctly summarizes that profound relationship between the Ten Commandments and Christ himself: "The people of Israel continue to be grateful to God because in the Commandments he pointed out the way of life. The great Psalm 119 (118) is a unique expression of joy for this fact: we are not fumbling in the dark. God has shown us the way and how to walk aright." Importantly, for us as followers of Christ, Pope Benedict states: "The message of the Commandments was synthesized in the life of Jesus and became a living model. Thus we understand that these rules from God are not chains, but the way which he is pointing out to us. We can be glad for them and rejoice that in Christ they stand before us as a lived reality. He himself has made us glad. By walking with Christ, we experience the joy of Revelation, and as priests we need to communicate to others our own joy at the fact that we have been shown the right way of life."

This is a challenge for priests and for all followers of Jesus as we seek to spell out the New Evangelization in a world seeking more and more the implications of the Gospel for our time. Those who have hope and faith live differently. The difference is not always apparent, and therein lies our daily challenge—to make the joy of our life in him more and more visible.

In the following chapters, I will follow a three-pronged approach in my analysis of each of the commandments:

1. What was the Jewish understanding of the commandment? Through a description of the text, I will examine how the commandment spoke to the ancient Israelites.

2. What effect did the Christ event have on the commandment in question? How did Christ fulfill it? The Sermon on the Mount will be helpful here. For example, the fifth commandment states: "You shall not kill." What Jesus says goes much further: "Everyone who grows angry with his brother shall be liable to judgment." There are many other examples of the effect of the Christ event.

3. What are some practical and pastoral implications of each commandment in our lives today? The *Catechism of the Catholic Church*; the *United States Catholic Catechism for Adults;* and two books by Alfred McBride, O. Praem., *The Ten Commandments: Sounds of Love from Sinai* and *The Ten Commandments: Covenant of Love,* will assist us here.

Reflect

1. What is one way, because of your faith, that you seek to live differently?

2. What steps do you take to inform your conscience when you are facing a difficult moral decision? How do you sort through the influence of popular culture and the media on the formation of your conscience?

3. St. Paul said, "I live, no longer I, but Christ lives in me." What do these words mean in your life?

Pray

O Lord, give me a mind
that is humble, quiet, peaceable,
patient and charitable,
and a taste of your Holy Spirit
in all my thoughts, words, and deeds.

O Lord, give me a lively faith, a firm hope,
a fervent charity, a love of you.
Take from me all lukewarmness in
    meditation
and all dullness in prayer.
Give me fervor and delight in thinking of
    you,
your grace, and your tender compassion
    toward me.

Give me, good Lord,
the grace to work for
the things we pray for.

—**St. Thomas More**

TWO

The First and Second Commandments: Liberating Words of Faith

The Ten Commandments are recorded twice in the Old Testament—once on Mount Sinai at the beginning of the Israelites' journey into the desert (Ex 20:1–17), and again just before their entry into Canaan at Mount Horeb (Dt 5:6–21) in a reminiscence of the experience of Sinai. These two mountain sites are often understood as two names for the same place but coming from different biblical traditions. In both traditions, the commandments are set forth on two stone tablets or tables. One tablet contains the first three commandments that focus on the love of God. The second tablet contains the other seven commandments whose focus is the love of neighbor. "The two tablets shed light on one another; they form an organic unity. . . . One cannot adore God without loving all men, his creatures" (CCC 2069). In this chapter, the subject is the first two commandments on the first tablet.

The First Commandment

I, the LORD, am your God, who brought you out of the land of Egypt, that place of slavery. You shall not have other gods besides me.

You shall not carve idols for yourselves in
the shape of anything in the sky above or on
the earth below or in the waters beneath the
earth; you shall not bow down before them
or worship them. For I, the LORD, your God,
am a jealous God, inflicting punishments for
their fathers' wickedness on the children of
those who hate me, down to the third and
fourth generation but bestowing mercy,
down to the thousandth generation, on the
children of those who love me and keep my
commandments. (Dt 5:6–10)

In our consideration of each of the commandments,
there is a common three-pronged approach—the Jewish
understanding of the commandment; the effect of the
Christ event on the commandment; and finally, some
practical and pastoral implications for our time.

The Jewish
Understanding of the Commandment

The first commandment flows directly from the Pro-
logue (Dt 5:6), that self-portrait of our God who identifies himself as the One who brought the chosen people
out of "that place of slavery." He is a God who brings
the Israelites to freedom and is linked to deliverance
from bondage. "The First Commandment calls us to
have faith in the true God, to hope in him, and to love
him fully with mind, heart, and will" (USCCA 341). Let
us look at the first commandment in sections:

"You shall not have other gods besides me."

The commandment expresses an exclusivity and a sense of the responsibility the Israelites bear in their covenant relationship with God. It is a responsibility of absolute faithfulness. The Israelites had already experienced the loving faithfulness of God toward them. He freed them from slavery. Now their response of faithfulness was demanded. It is an exclusive and total allegiance to their God. He brooks no rivals—no "other gods besides me."

These "other gods" are those remembered from Egypt and those to be encountered in the Promised Land. Sixty-four times "other gods" are mentioned in the Old Testament. The Israelites had known their God in the Exodus and had sensed his presence in the desert. But would they also be able to find him, his presence, in the new lifestyle they were about to adopt in the Promised Land? That is the challenge of the first commandment. Their God had already proven his loving faithfulness. Now it was their turn to show their fidelity to him. After they had left the desert and entered the Promised Land, the Israelites would have encountered the Canaanite fertility gods as they became farmers in the Promised Land. The fertility cult would have been difficult to avoid, and that is why the Lord gave them this first commandment. The first commandment calls for a style of life dominated by a relationship to God. It affects the whole life of a whole covenant community. It affects every aspect of life, action, thought, and emotion. It is at the foundation of the biblical understanding of religion itself.

"You shall not carve idols for yourselves . . . you shall not bow down before them or worship them."

Prohibition of idols included images that in some physical way are intended to represent God. That was the prohibition. No "created" image does legitimate service to a "living" God. That is the point. God communicated himself, revealed himself, indeed identified himself in two ways—by action (delivering his people from slavery) *and* by his voice (the Lord "spoke" to his people on Sinai). He did not reveal himself in images. That would have restricted and indeed limited the transcendent, living, and dynamic nature of our God. That would be too static. No idol can capture a living God, the God who revealed himself to the Israelites. No cultic representation can do justice to a living God. The first commandment liberated the Israelites so that they could have an exclusive faith in a living God.

"For I, the Lord, your God, am a jealous God . . ."

How do we understand the concept of jealousy? Does that not have a pejorative or negative connotation? Understood properly, however, it is God's way of saying that he will have nothing less than our full devotion, and we will have nothing less than his full love. Oh, the sounds of love coming from Mount Sinai! It is the kind of attribute that belongs to a marriage relationship where there is a proper covenantal jealousy between husband and wife. It is a "holy" jealousy of God for his children. He created us. He loves us. He wants us for himself. He knows what is harmful to us. He is aware of what is capable of separating us from him and from his love. His kind of jealousy is not restrictive, mean, nor cruel. It is an infinite love and infinite goodness.

"Bestowing mercy, down to the thousandth generation."

Finally, God speaks of punishments for those who hate him, down to the third and fourth generation. But significantly, he speaks, in the same breath, of bestowing mercy down to the thousandth generation "on the children of those who love me and keep my commandments." The implication of these expressions for understanding God's expectation and God's nature is clear. Our God is "rich in mercy." The scales are tipped; the divine character is weighted toward mercy, the restorative power of God. Love and mercy, to the thousandth generation, are his dominant characteristics. The first commandment reveals to the Israelites, and to us, a God who demands exclusive obedience and love; a God who cannot be captured by idols; a God who is jealous for our love, but with a proven track record of total, merciful, and complete love for his children.

The Effect of the Christ Event on the Commandment

After God had spoken many times and in various way through the prophets, "in these last days he has spoken to us by a Son" (Heb 1:1–2). For he sent his Son, the eternal Word, who enlightens all men, to dwell among men and to tell them about the inner life of God (cf. Jn 1:1–18). Hence, Jesus Christ, sent as "a man to men," "speaks the words of God" (Jn 3:34), and accomplishes the saving work which the Father gave him to do (cf. Jn 5:36; 17:4). As a result, he himself—to see whom is to see the Father (Jn 14:9)—completed and perfected Revelation and confirmed it with divine guarantees. He did this by the total fact of his presence and self-manifestation— by words and works, signs and miracles, but above all by his death and glorious resurrection from the dead and finally by sending the Spirit of truth. He revealed that God was with us, to deliver us from the darkness of sin and death, and to raise us up to eternal life. (*DV* 4)

In Jesus Christ, the God who was revealed to Moses and who jealously seeks total and exclusive faithfulness becomes fully revealed to us. To see him is to see the Father and to contemplate the face of God. Jesus Christ is both the revealer and the revealed. The Christ event completes and perfects that which was revealed by our God on Mount Sinai in the first commandment. It is the same Jesus who, after being tempted in the desert for the third time, said to Satan—recalling the first commandment: "The Lord, your God, shall you worship and him alone shall you serve" (Mt 4:10). Furthermore, "the Christian veneration of images is not contrary to the first commandment which proscribes idols. . . . The honor paid to sacred images is a 'respectful veneration,' not the adoration due to God alone" (*CCC* 2132).

In Jesus Christ, we can know about our God in more specific ways. Like the God of Mount Sinai, he, too, speaks and acts in history. Speaking/acting and words/

deeds remain his identifying characteristics. He is a living God.

Jesus, in words and deeds, fully reveals the God who spoke in the first commandment, for "he is the image of the invisible God" (Col 1:15). He also makes it possible for us, reborn in the grace of Baptism, to become children of the invisible God. He makes it possible for us to carry him within us and to live his law in a new way. Now, the divine law, once written on stone tablets, has also been written on the human heart. Remember the words of Ezekiel: "I will give you a new heart and place a new spirit within you, taking from your bodies your stony hearts and giving you natural hearts. I will put my spirit within you and make you live by my statutes, careful to observe my decrees" (Ez 36:26–27).

That new spirit is the Spirit of Jesus Christ. It is the life of his Holy Spirit, the treasure in earthen vessels, that makes it possible for us to know our God, to hear his voice, and to live his commandments. "The way we may be sure that we know him is to keep his commandments" (1 Jn 2:3). It is in the doing that we come to know Jesus. And that is possible because of the Holy Spirit living within us.

Some Practical and Pastoral Implications

Is God, the God who is fully revealed by and in Jesus Christ, the foundation of our lives, our faith, our prayer? That is the question put to us by the first commandment—"to have no other gods besides me." In the words of Deuteronomy 6 (the Shema), do we really heed the Lord's command: "You shall love the Lord, your God, with all your heart, and with all your

soul, and with all your strength" (Dt 6:4–5)? This then
is foundational—foundational to our relationship with
Jesus Christ in the power of the Holy Spirit.

During Benedict XVI's historic visit to Washington on April 16, 2008, in his address to the bishops, he
warned against materialism in our nation. Materialism can become a competing god to the God we know
and love. "For an affluent society," he said, "a further
obstacle to an encounter with the living God lies in the
subtle influence of materialism . . . at the expense of
the eternal life which he promises in the age to come."
One practical example that we have seen in our time is
the negative consequences of excessive borrowing and
the irresponsible use of credit. It is as if one need not
even repay what is borrowed. Encouraged by television
advertisements, such a way of life can lead, and has led,
to an undue worship of material goods. The Pope also
points out that "secularism can . . . color the way people allow their faith to influence their behavior." It can
become a competing god. It leads to the question: "Is it
consistent to profess our beliefs in church on Sunday,
and then during the week to promote business practices
or medical procedures contrary to those beliefs?" Our
faith must permeate every aspect of our lives. It is faith
in a living God alone and what he reveals and teaches.

Our world is increasingly one of pressure for
increased billable hours, patients, and clients; count-
less meetings, income, clout, and connections; powerful
positions; the demands of instant communications; and
prestigious offices and titles. Each of these, and maybe
even work itself, can become a god unto itself if we are
not careful.

The first commandment challenges us to live an examined life, to identify the driving forces that captivate our motivations and impel our actions. They are unique to each of us. Is Jesus our driving force? Is our response, our worship of him, made concrete every day in prayer? For Christians, praying is as essential as breathing. Or do we make ourselves and other material objects our god?

In Paris on September 13, 2008, Benedict XVI also spoke about the first commandment's rejection of idols:

> This appeal to shun idols, dear brothers and sisters, is also pertinent today. Has not our modern world created its own idols? Has it not imitated, perhaps inadvertently, the pagans of antiquity, by diverting man from his true end, from the joy of living eternally with God? This is a question that all people, if they are honest with themselves, cannot help but ask. What is important in my life? What is my first priority? The word "idol" comes from the Greek and means "image," "figure," "representation," but also "ghost," "phantom," "vain appearance." An idol is a delusion, for it turns its worshipper away from reality and places him in the kingdom of mere appearances. Now, is this not a temptation in our own day? It is the temptation to idolize a past that no longer exists, forgetting its shortcomings; it is the temptation to idolize a future which does not yet exist, in the belief that, by his efforts alone, man can bring about the kingdom of eternal joy on earth! Saint Paul explains

to the Colossians that insatiable greed is a
form of idolatry (cf. 3:5), and he reminds
his disciple Timothy that love of money
is the root of all evil. By yielding to it, he
explains, "some people in their desire for it
have strayed from the faith and have pierced
themselves with many pains" (1 Tm 6:10).
Have not money, the thirst for possessions,
for power and even for knowledge, diverted
man from his true destiny?

I might add that even certain sports, when followed
to the neglect of faith and family, can become idols. An
examined life helps prevent this.

Alfred McBride offers this fitting insight to conclude
our look at the first commandment:

Correcting untrue meanings about the
real God—abandoning false gods—is
only one aspect of the teaching of the First
Commandment. Equally important is the
positive effort to perceive the real God:
caring, forgiving, loving, challenging and
actively nourishing our free participation
in the work of salvation. God asks us to
find out who God really is, to embark on a
lifelong faith journey.

The first commandment is thus God's liberating
voice inviting us to faith in him and him alone.

The Second Commandment

"You shall not take the name of the Lord, your God, in vain. For the Lord will not leave unpunished him who takes his name in vain" (Dt 5:11).

The Jewish Understanding of the Commandment

The second commandment has often been taken, on its face, as a prohibition against blasphemy, i.e., words of hatred, reproach, or defiance against God. Such an interpretation, although certainly a part of the commandment's meaning, is too narrow. Instead, the commandment is concerned with the name of God, respect for the sacredness of his personal name—Yahweh ("I am who am")—that gives some clue to the intimacy of the covenant relationship. For the name of the Lord is holy.

In the ancient Near East, the name of a person or God was considered to contain certain implicit power: for example, a Moabite king sought to use the name *Balaam* to curse the Israelites magically in the name of the Lord (Nm 22:4–6). Thus, one of the purposes of the commandment was to proscribe the use of God's name in magic, which was an explicit attempt to harness God's power for personal ends. In fact, any attempt to manipulate God for personal gain comes under the prohibition.

In scripture, generally, the name of a thing or person indicates much more than our typical understanding of it. "A name in some way conveys the reality of a person—the origin, the history, the very being of the person" (*USCCA* 354). To know someone's name means to penetrate into the reality of a person. It is not simply the appellation of an individual. It is so much more. The change of a name, for example, means a change of that person's very identity or mission in life. The name *Abram* was changed by God to *Abraham* (Father of the Multitude); *Sarai* was changed to *Sarah* (Princess); *Jacob* became *Israel* (One Who Contends with God).

It is clear in the Old Testament that the use of the name of God played an important role in Israel's faith from the very beginning. One "called" on the name; "prophesied" in the name of; "blessed" the name; "praised," "trusted," "sought refuge" in the name. On the other hand, the misuse of a name remained a continuing threat. It was forbidden to profane God's name, to blaspheme, to curse, to defile, to abuse, and to swear falsely.

For sure, then, this early prohibition of the misuse of God's name sought to protect the divine name. It was an attempt to protect the very nature of a loving God who out of love had entered a covenantal relationship with his people.

The Effect of the Christ Event on the Commandment

In the Sermon on the Mount, Jesus teaches: "Again you have heard that it was said to your ancestors, 'Do not take a false oath, but make good to the Lord all that you vow.' But I say to you, do not swear at all" (Mt 5:33–34). "Jesus teaches that every oath involves a reference to God and that God's presence and his truth must be honored in all speech" (*CCC* 2153). There is, after all, a holiness to the divine name.

The name *Jesus*, at which "every knee should bend, of those in heaven and on earth and under the earth" (Phil 2:10), comes from the Hebrew *Yeshua* (Joshua), which means "Yahweh saves." Here again, the name reveals the nature. In Jesus, God saves. "Jesus taught that he would be present to those who come together in his name. 'Where two or three are gathered together in my name, there am I in the midst of them' (Mt 18:20)" (*USCCA* 357).

"In the name of Jesus Christ the Nazarean, [rise and] walk" (Acts 3:6). With these words, Peter took hold of a beggar who had been lame from birth and lifted him to his feet. The surprised man had no choice but to stand. He began to praise God, jumping and dancing. But the crowd needed an explanation. Peter addressed them: "Why are you amazed at this, and why do you look so intently at us as if we had made him walk by our own power or piety? . . . By faith in [Jesus'] name, this man, whom you see and know, his name has made strong . . ." (Acts 3:12). The name of Jesus healed the man.

The name of Jesus has miraculous power. St. Bernard of Clairvaux wrote that the name of Jesus has the three-fold property of oil: it illuminates, it nourishes, and it anoints. When preached, it gives light. When meditated upon, it nourishes. When invoked, it alleviates the wounds of mind and soul. In his name, we are made whole again.

Some Practical and Pastoral Implications

At Baptism, each of us is given a name, a name for all eternity, a name by which God calls us. Quoting canon law, the Catechism teaches: "Parents, sponsors, and the pastor are to see that a name is not given which is foreign to Christian sentiment" (*CCC* 2156). It is most often the name of a saint, one who has lived an exemplary Christian life. A Christian name is another way to break down the barrier between our aggressively secular society and the call to holiness that belongs to each of us. For in a Christian name, we actually come in contact with the holy. In addition, "to be baptized in the name of the Trinity means to be immersed into the very life of the Father, Son, and Spirit. God's name sanctifies us" (*USCCA* 354).

It is thus too simplistic to see the second commandment as only a prohibition against using the Lord's name in vain. It means more than that. It calls for a reverence and respect for the sacredness of the name of God. When we bow our heads at the name of Jesus, we show respect for his name and honor the second commandment. When we share his name and share his life with others, we show a respect and reverence for him.

And it takes courage to speak the name of Jesus. How often, if at all, do we speak the name of Jesus in the workplace or at home, to a spouse, child, or friend? Am I afraid or embarrassed to mention the name of Jesus in public or among friends? For an example of courage, consider the responsory for the feast of Sts. Peter and Paul: "They gave us their lives for the name of our Lord Jesus Christ." That is the ultimate Christian witness. Do we give up our lives for his name, even in little ways?

Reflect on the holiness of his name and the liberating word of holiness found in the second commandment. In the Our Father, we pray "Hallowed be your name." In the Magnificat, we pray "From this day all generations will call me blessed: the Almighty has done great things for me, and holy is his name." And from the Benediction hymn, we sing: "Holy God we praise thy Name." In Psalm 8, we pray "O Lord, our Lord, how glorious is your name over all the earth."

Reflect

1. What gods, if any, compete with the one true God in your life?

2. How is it true (or not true) for you that it takes courage to speak the name of Jesus?

3. How do you try to put in practice the greatest commandment: "You shall love the Lord, your God, with all your heart, and with all your soul, and with all your strength" (Dt 6:4–5)?

Pray

Dear God, you are indeed the one true God. You are the Creator of Heaven and Earth. The King of kings and Lord of lords. You alone are my Rock and my Redeemer.

You know, Lord, that no other "god" in my life displaces you. But there are times when my loyalty is split, when I "worship" other gods. There are times I find it hard to surrender everything to you. I want to hang on to that which gives me safety and control. Forgive me, dear Lord, when I allow other "gods" into your presence.

Help me, by your grace and through your Spirit, to have no other "god" in your presence. May my covenant relationship with you be exclusive in every way. May I put my full trust in you and you alone. And may I live for you each moment of each day, no matter what I'm doing.

To you be all the glory, gracious and glorious God! Amen.

—**Mark D. Roberts**

THREE

The Third Commandment:
A Day Set Aside for
Love of God

How can we demonstrate our love for God in a better way than by keeping holy the Lord's Day, the focus of the third commandment?

The Jewish
Understanding of the Commandment

To understand the depth of this commandment for the Jewish people, it is important to compare the text from Exodus with that of Deuteronomy. Consider first the text from Exodus:

> Remember to keep holy the sabbath day. Six days you may labor and do all your work, but the seventh day is the sabbath of the LORD, your God. No work may be done then either by you, or your son or daughter, or your male or female slave, or your beast, or by the alien who lives with you. In six days the LORD made the heavens and the earth, the sea and all that is in them; but on the seventh day he rested. That is why the LORD

has blessed the sabbath day and made it
holy. (Ex 20:8–11)

Now compare the text of the same commandment
in Deuteronomy:

Take care to keep holy the sabbath day as
the LORD, your God, commanded you. Six
days you may labor and do all your work;
but the seventh day is the sabbath of the
LORD, your God. No work may be done then,
whether by you, or your son or daughter, or
your male or female slave, or your ox or ass
or any of your beasts, or the alien who lives
with you. Your male and female slave should
rest as you do. For remember that you too
were once slaves in Egypt, and the LORD,
your God, brought you from there with his
strong hand and outstretched arm. That is
why the LORD, your God, has commanded
you to observe the sabbath day. (Dt 5:12–15)

In Exodus, the first text, we are told that God created
the world in six days and on the seventh he rested. The
seventh was the Sabbath. The Jews kept this day holy
because on it God stopped creating for a time, and they
join him in that period of rest. Exodus is thus linked to
the creation. And the Sabbath is thus a rest from creation, from our participation in the creative activity of
God. Of course, "it would be banal to interpret God's
'rest' as a kind of divine 'inactivity'" (*DD* 10). God's
creative power is unceasing. In effect, God engages in
a kind of contemplative gaze on all he has done. So
for Jews, and for us, the commandment highlights rest

from our human creative activity so that we do not idolize work and make it into a god.

In contrast, the text of the same commandment from Deuteronomy underscores that the Lord's Day is a memorial of Israel's liberation from bondage in Egypt. "For remember that you too were once slaves in Egypt, and the Lord, your God, brought you from there with his strong hand and outstretched arm. That is why the Lord, your God, has commanded you to observe the sabbath day" (Dt 5:12–15). God entrusted the sabbath to Israel to keep as a *"sign of the irrevocable covenant"* (CCC 2171).

The emphasis here is not on a rest from creation and the need to contemplate what humans have created, but a rest from the oppression of unrelenting human labor. There is an identification with a slave in need of rest. In breaking free from labor, the Israelites were challenged to remember God's breaking them free from the hard toil and bondage in Egypt.

Creation and liberation are distinct yet closely linked.

> The God who rests on the seventh day, rejoicing in his creation, is the same God who reveals his glory in liberating his children from the Pharaoh's oppression. . . . As certain elements of the same Jewish tradition suggest, to reach the heart of the *"shabbat,"* of God's "rest," we need to recognize in both the Old and the New Testament the nuptial intensity which marks the relationship between God and his people. (*DD* 12)

God's incredible love for his people echoes from Mount Sinai, a love that was at the heart of the Jewish understanding of the third commandment—and of all the commandments.

The Effect of the Christ Event on the Commandment

For Christians, Sunday replaced the Sabbath. "This tradition goes back to the time of the Apostles" (*USCCA* 364). "The sabbath, which represented the completion of the first creation, has been replaced by Sunday which recalls the new creation inaugurated by the Resurrection of Christ" (*CCC* 2190). The resurrection recalls the final and liberating victory of Christ over sin and death. Both the creation and liberation themes, found in the Jewish understanding of Sabbath rest, are carried over in a new, unique, and definitive way as a result of Christ's death and resurrection.

"In fact, in the weekly reckoning of time, Sunday recalls the day of Christ's Resurrection. It is Easter which returns week by week, celebrating Christ's victory over sin and death, the fulfillment in him of the first creation and the dawn of 'the new creation'" (*DD* 1). The Resurrection of Jesus is the fundamental event upon which Christian faith rests. Sunday is thus at the heart and soul of every Christian's spirituality.

In the beautiful Easter readings, scripture reveals the importance of that "first day of the week." In the gospel texts of Matthew, Mark, Luke, and John, we read accounts of the discovery of the empty tomb—each with a little different twist. But what they have in common is that the visit of the holy women at the tomb always takes place "on the first day of the week" (Mt 28:1; Mk 16:2, 9; Lk 24:1; Jn 20:1). Sunday is the first day after the Sabbath. Remember also that most beautiful account of the journey to Emmaus. This also takes place on "that very day" (Sunday) when the risen Lord joined the two disciples on the road. Their hearts were burning when he broke open the scripture to them, and they ultimately came to know him in the breaking of the bread (Lk 24:13–35). Then again, the risen Lord appeared to the eleven in the upper room "on the evening of that first day of the week" (Jn 20:19; Lk 24:36).

Pope Benedict underscored the importance of the Jewish Sabbath and Christ's own reverence for it in his day. Speaking about the relations between Christians and Jews to a Jewish group on his visit to Paris, the Pope said:

> It is a happy circumstance that our meeting takes place on the eve of the weekly celebration of "Shabbat," the day that since time immemorial occupies such an outstanding place in the religious and cultural life of the people of Israel. Every pious Jew sanctifies the "Shabbat" by reading the Scriptures and reciting the psalms. Dear friends, as you know, Jesus' prayer was also nourished by the psalms. He went regularly to the Temple and to the synagogue. He spoke there on the Sabbath day. (September 12, 2008)

As the Catechism says: "In Christ's Passover, Sunday fulfills the spiritual truth of the Jewish sabbath and announces our eternal rest in God" (CCC 2175).

Some Practical and Pastoral Implications

But what should we do on Sunday? How then should we spend our Sundays if Sunday is the heart of our spirituality? First and foremost, it is the Day of the Lord, a day set aside for love of God. What does this mean for those of us who are constantly connected through a myriad of electronic devices? The Catechism reminds us: "Keeping the Lord's Day holy can serve as a helpful corrective for a 'consumer' society that tends to place value on people for their productivity and material possessions" (*USCCA* 368).

Three points come to mind immediately. They are the basis of our late Holy Father John Paul II's Apostolic Letter, *The Day of the Lord (Dies Domini)*; and part of the Apostolic Letter of Pope Benedict XVI, *The Sacrament of Charity (Sacramentum Caritatis)*.

- The Eucharist is the heart of Sunday.
- Sunday has been a day of rest from the earliest times.
- Sunday is a day to spend with family and friends and in acts of charity.

The Eucharist Is the Heart of Sunday

For us, Sunday should be a day of prayer and rest. Attendance at Mass on Sunday is not optional for Catholics. The Catechism, citing canon law, clearly states: "On Sundays and other holy days of obligation the faithful are bound to participate in the Mass" (*CCC* 2180).

In *The Sacrament of Charity* Benedict XVI writes:

> The life of faith is endangered when we lose the desire to share in the celebration of the

Eucharist and its commemoration of the paschal victory. Participating in the Sunday liturgical assembly with all our brothers and sisters, with whom we form one body in Jesus Christ, is demanded by our Christian conscience and at the same time it forms that conscience. To lose a sense of Sunday as the Lord's Day, a day to be sanctified, is symptomatic of the loss of an authentic sense of Christian freedom, the freedom of the children of God. (*SC* 73)

Many reasons are given, some good and some bad, for the decrease in Sunday Mass attendance. Nonetheless, there is reason for hope in our country. The *United States Catholic Catechism for Adults* notes: "There are more Catholics at Mass on a single weekend than all the fans that go to major league baseball games in the entire season" (*USCCA* 370).

The more we understand the great gift of the Eucharist and the more we are nourished and strengthened by the Word of God, the more likely we are to participate "fully, actively and consciously" in Sunday Mass as well as during the week. A whole new catechesis is required. We need to prepare for Mass as we would prepare for anything else worthwhile in our lives.

Why is this especially true for Sunday? Because of its special solemnity and the obligatory presence of the whole Catholic community. "Each community, gathering all its members for the 'breaking of the bread,' becomes the place where the mystery of the Church is concretely made present" (*DD* 34). There is an old saying that the Church makes the Eucharist and the Eucharist makes the Church. That happens at holy Mass and on Sunday in particular. The Eucharist is the heart of Sunday and an indispensable element of our identity as Catholics.

The resurrection is the beginning of a new creation. That is what we ponder on Sunday. It is a day of faith. It is a day "when by the power of the Holy Spirit (first given us on Sunday) who is the Church's living 'memory,' the first appearance of the Risen Lord becomes an event renewed in the 'today' of each of Christ's disciples" (*DD* 29). For each of us, Sunday "is an indispensable element of our Christian identity" (*DD* 30). And for all of these reasons, it should be clear why Sunday Mass is obligatory not so much under the penalty of sin but out of a desire to share with each other at least once per week the "memory" of the greatest victory of love the world has ever known.

Sunday Is a Day of Rest

Sunday should also be a day of grace and rest from work after the model of God, who rested on the seventh day. All unnecessary work should be avoided. This is not easy for most of us. The Second Vatican Council teaches that "the institution of Sunday helps all 'to be allowed sufficient rest and leisure to cultivate their familial, cultural, social, and religious lives'" (*CCC* 2194).

Pope Benedict writes:

> It is particularly urgent nowadays to remember that the day of the Lord is also a day of rest from work. It is greatly to be hoped that this fact will also be recognized by civil society, so that individuals can be permitted to refrain from work without

being penalized. Christians, not without reference to the meaning of the Sabbath in the Jewish tradition, have seen in the Lord's Day a day of rest from their daily exertions. This is highly significant, for it relativizes work and directs it to the person: work is for man and not man for work. It is easy to see how this actually protects men and women, emancipating them from a possible form of enslavement. As I have had occasion to say, "work is of fundamental importance to the fulfillment of the human being and to the development of society . . . it is indispensable that people not allow themselves to be enslaved by work or to idolize it, claiming to find in it the ultimate and definitive meaning of life. It is on the day consecrated to God that men and women come to understand the meaning of their lives and also of their work." (SC 74)

Sunday rest has biblical roots, as we have seen. We know from the creation accounts that God rested on the seventh day. In the third commandment, he ordered, not simply suggested, that we keep holy the Sabbath day. It is a day blessed by God. It is God's day. He also links the Sabbath day with the act of remembering. In the Exodus account, we read: "For remember that you too were once slaves in Egypt, and the Lord, your God, brought you from there with his strong hand and outstretched arm. That is why the Lord, your God, has commanded you to observe the sabbath day" (Dt 5:15).

Can you see the link to Sunday? God commands the Israelites to keep the Sabbath holy by remembering the greatest of the saving works he accomplished for them—delivery from slavery. For us as Christians, "what God accomplished in creation and wrought for his people in the Exodus has found its fullest expression in Christ's Death and Resurrection" (DD 18). We remember that fundamental mystery of our faith on Sunday. And that requires "rest" in the Lord so that we keep his day holy and sacred.

This is a big challenge. No longer are there laws that prohibit commerce on Sunday. In fact, for many, Sunday becomes a day of shopping. For those with families and children, Sunday becomes a day of one sports game after another. "We must preserve the opportunity to go to Mass on Sundays without competition from sporting events, work, or other temptations" (USCCA 369). In a pastoral letter to his archdiocese, Archbishop Timothy Dolan of New York addressed the threats to Sunday observance from children's sports and other activities and the primacy of Sunday Mass: "There is no denying that this will occasion some sacrifice, but the development of a child is not well served by indicating that Sunday Mass is secondary to other things." Another threat to the primacy of Sunday involves those who are overburdened at work. For them, Sunday becomes a day to catch up at the office or prepare for the week—a day of work, not rest.

And yet, God commands us to keep Sunday holy. We simply cannot ignore his revealed word. This is perhaps as challenging as some of the other supposedly more difficult commandments for us. "Through Sunday rest, daily concerns and tasks can find their proper perspective: the material things about which we worry give way to spiritual values; in a moment of encounter and less pressured exchange, we see the true face of the people with whom we live" (*DD* 67). What a wonderful insight! How often do we simply live with our spouses and children or close friends whose busyness prevents us from truly coming to know them as individuals? Sunday rest gives us that necessary opportunity.

"Rest is something 'sacred' because it is man's way of withdrawing from the sometimes excessively demanding cycle of earthly tasks in order to renew his awareness that everything is the work of God" (*DD* 65). Note well that "there is a risk that the prodigious power over creation which God gives to man can lead him to forget that God is the Creator upon whom everything depends" (*DD* 65).

On the seventh day, God rested, and so must we. Sunday is the day of the new creation. It is our Sabbath. Sunday is the day for Christians to remember not the exodus, but the salvation that comes to us in Baptism and has made us new in Christ by Christ's death and resurrection. At the same time, Sunday is more than a replacement for the Sabbath. It is its fulfillment, and in a certain sense, its extension and fullest expression in the ordered unfolding of salvation history, which reaches its climax in the resurrection of Jesus Christ, the new creation.

Sunday Is a Day for Acts of Charity

"To experience the joy of the Risen Lord deep within is to share fully the love which pulses in his heart: there is no joy without love" (*DD* 69). The Sunday Eucharist commits us to acts of charity and love. The challenge to love is what the dismissal means when we are told at the end of the Eucharist to go and live the Mass. The

Eucharist is an eloquent sign of a total and free and generous love. It offers each of us the joy of the Lord's presence within us that makes it possible for us to love all the more after his example. In fact, Pope Benedict boldly writes: "A Eucharist which does not pass over into the concrete practice of love is intrinsically fragmented" (*DCE* 14).

The Eucharist signifies an actual principle of life from which love results. It communicates the strength to imitate Christ's life in our own lives. Through the Eucharist, his love comes to take over our very hearts in order that we might be committed more resolutely to the path of charity.

From the earliest apostolic times, the Sunday gathering has, in fact, been for Christians a moment of sharing with the poor. "On the first day of the week, each of you is to put aside and save whatever extra you earn" (1 Cor 16:2). St. Paul refers here to the collection for the poor churches in Judea. St. John Chrysostom writes:

> Do you wish to honor the body of Christ? Do not ignore him when he is naked. Do not pay him homage in the temple clad in silk only then to neglect him outside when he suffers cold and nakedness. He who said: "This is my body" is the same One who said: "You saw me hungry and you gave me no food," and "Whatever you did to the least of my brothers you did also to me." . . . What good is it if the Eucharistic table is overloaded with golden chalices, when he is dying of hunger? Start by satisfying his hunger, and then with what is left you may adorn the altar as well. (*DD* 71)

The Lord's Day is quite explicit about how we are to live the Sunday Eucharist. "If Sunday is a day of joy, Christians should declare by their actual behavior that we cannot be happy 'on our own'" (*DD* 72). On Sunday we should seek out people who may need help. We may know a sick or a lonely elderly person in our neighborhood, or immigrants who on Sunday feel their isolation more keenly. It is true that our commitment to these people cannot be restricted to an occasional Sunday gesture. But presuming a wider sense of commitment, why not make the Lord's Day a more intense time of sharing and encouraging with all the inventiveness of which Christian charity is capable? It might mean inviting people who are alone to a meal, visiting the sick, providing food for needy families, and spending a few hours in voluntary work and acts of solidarity. These would certainly be ways of bringing into needy people's lives the love of Christ received at the Eucharistic table. It might mean also bringing the Eucharist on Sunday to some housebound person.

Lived in this way, not only the Sunday Eucharist but the whole of Sunday becomes a great school of charity, justice, and peace. The presence of the risen Lord in the midst of his people becomes an undertaking of solidarity, a compelling force for inner renewal, an inspiration to change the structures of sin in which individuals, communities, and at times entire peoples are entangled. Far from being an escape, the Christian Sunday is a "prophecy" inscribed on time itself, a prophecy obliging the faithful to follow in the footsteps of the One who came "to bring glad tidings to the poor. He has sent me to proclaim liberty to the captives and recovery of sight to the blind, to let the oppressed go free, and to proclaim a year acceptable to the Lord" (Lk 4:18–19). In the Sunday commemoration of Easter, believers learn from Christ; and remembering his promise: "Peace I leave with you; my peace I give to you" (Jn 14:27), they become in their turn builders of peace.

The third commandment, to keep holy the Lord's Day, thus has clear implications for those of us who follow Jesus. Sunday, the Lord's Day, the day of the resurrection, is at the heart and soul of the spirituality of each follower of Jesus. The Eucharist, rest, and charitable solidarity! There can be no better formula to discover the risen Lord in our lives and to share his love with others. Is that not what our faith is all about? Is not Sunday, in effect, a synthesis of the entire Christian life? Hopefully, this chapter will challenge you, as it does me, to examine your own life and the role Sunday, the focus of the third commandment, presently plays in your spirituality. You might even decide to make some adjustments in how you will spend Sunday in the future. Easter Sunday is, after all, not the only day in the year for a family Sunday brunch or get-together. Every Sunday is a celebration of Easter—a day of the Eucharist, rest, and works of charity—a day set apart in love for the Lord.

Reflect

1. What do you or could you do to try to make Sunday a day of rest?

2. What are some ways that you have reached out or could reach out to others in need on a Sunday?

3. How does or might "keeping Sunday holy" make a difference in your life?

Pray

The Lord is my shepherd;
there is nothing I lack.
In green pastures you let me graze;
to safe waters you lead me;
you restore my strength.
You guide me along the right path
for the sake of your name.
Even when I walk through a dark valley,
I fear no harm for you are at my side;
your rod and staff give me courage.
You set a table before me as my enemies
watch;
You anoint my head with oil; my cup
overflows.
Only goodness and love will pursue me
all the days of my life;
I will dwell in the house of the Lord
for years to come.

—Psalm 23

FOUR

The Fourth Commandment: Love for Mother and Father— An Unfolding Love

A few years ago, a friend and I visited the Borghese Museum in Rome. It is a wonderful museum set in the Borghese Gardens in the heart of the city. In particular fashion, we were both struck by a statue of Aeneas fleeing from the burning Troy. In this magnificent piece of art by Gian Lorenzo Bernini, Aeneas is carrying his father on his shoulders, and his little son is clinging to him as they escape Troy. Aeneas, a prince of Troy and the son of Venus, became a part of pre-Roman history when he escaped from the destruction of Troy with his son and father. He dutifully followed the destiny set down by the gods, earning the name *pius* Aeneas, and eventually led the surviving Trojans to settle in the area that would become Rome.

Aeneas exhibited all the characteristics necessary for a great hero: selflessness, honor, loyalty, and *pietas*. *Pietas* is a traditional Roman value that can be defined as "duty, honor, and responsibility to others," and the taking of these obligations seriously. Throughout antiquity, Aeneas was associated with this Roman value of *pietas*. And the statue in Rome has forever been a part of my memory when I think of the fourth commandment.

In our day, the fourth commandment is not simply about young children honoring parents. It includes the value of *pietas* and prescribes taking care of our parents, especially—but not only—as they grow older. As Aeneas rescued his father, exhibiting so well the virtue of *pietas*, each of us is called to show duty and honor to our parents and teach our children to do the same. It is a love unfolding. Keep this image of Aeneas in mind as we study the fourth commandment. This commandment applies to all of us, no matter our age or circumstances. Referring to this commandment, the Catechism teaches: "It likewise concerns the ties of kinship between members of the extended family. It requires honor, affection, and gratitude toward elders and ancestors" (*CCC* 2199). I think most especially of a young parishioner of mine who helps his grandmother with such love and care every Sunday as he assists her into church, walking arm in arm. What a beautiful way to embrace the fourth commandment! It is a commandment, after all, that deals with the family and requires that we honor our father and mother and grandparents. It is about "family values" and the value of the family as the "domestic church." It speaks moreover of relationships within a family. We begin this chapter where we always do, namely, with the Jewish understanding of the fourth commandment.

The Jewish Understanding of the Commandment

There are two major points to underscore here—the linkage of the fourth commandment to the covenant with Moses, and the fourth commandment seen as a bridge between the first three commandments and the other six. The commandment reads: "Honor your father and your mother, that you may have a long life in the land which the LORD, your God, is giving you" (Ex 20:12).

First, at the heart of the Jewish understanding of "parental honor" is the link to the covenant. Remember that the Ten Commandments were at the core of the covenant relationship between the Lord and the Israelites. They were the way free people were to live. The texts both from Deuteronomy and Exodus link the command to honor father and mother with the promise of "a long life" and prosperity "in the land which the LORD, your God, is giving you."

In Israelite culture, parents were obliged to teach their children about the covenant. By so doing, parents, as well as their children, would prosper in the land promised them. Parents were the repositories of tradition, and they thus deserved respect and honor from their children. If parents were to teach effectively, children had to be a receptive audience. If children did not honor their parents and were rebellious and self-centered, they would not be able to learn the key covenant relationship with God; and as a consequence of dishonoring their parents, children would not prosper in the Promised Land. The fruit of children honoring parents in this way was a solid family structure for the Israelites and the passing on of the "charter of freedom."

No penalties were set forth nor threats attached for failure to comply with the fourth commandment, but other passages in the Old Testament underscore that this commandment was among the weightiest. In particular, Sirach 3:1–16 is akin to a commentary on the fourth commandment. In part, it reads: "He who honors his father atones for sins; he stores up riches who reveres his mother. He who honors his father is gladdened by children, and when he prays he is heard. He who reveres his father will live a long life; he obeys the LORD who brings comfort to his mother" (Sir 3:3–6). (Read also Dt 21:18–21; Prv 19:26, 20:20, 30:17; Lv 20:9).

Another aspect of the Jewish understanding of this commandment concerns its nature as a bridge. The first three commandments are traditionally understood as being about our obligations to God, whereas the second seven treat obligations toward fellow human beings. But scripture scholars point out that the reference to the "Lord, your God" in the fourth commandment serves as a bridge between those commandments traditionally understood as relating to God and those relating to one's fellow human beings.

Another argument, in addition to the explicit use of the word *God*, is the use of the word *honor (kabbed)*—a word traditionally used in relation to God. *Honor* or *kabbed* frequently has God as its object. To honor parents, in the Jewish mentality, is thus to accord them a respect and importance typically reserved for the sacred. In effect, parents become visible representatives of God. The commandment thus suggests an attitude toward parents that parallels one's attitude toward God—honor, fear, and reverence.

The Greeks and Romans were just as convinced as the Jews that honor must be paid to parents. In his *Nicomachean Ethics*, Aristotle writes: "Honor is also due to the parents as it is to the gods."

Note well that the fourth commandment uses the Hebrew word *kabbed* that is translated "honor," rather than the Hebrew word for "obey." This is not accidental. The duty of obedience diminishes as children become adults. But honor can and should persist long after the age of dependence. People are always the children of their parents, and their obligation does not cease as long as the parents live. That is the point. By showing honor to their parents, children strengthen the system that bestows honor on themselves as parents, even when a kind of role reversal is taking place as our parents age and as we, too, age.

The fourth commandment is admittedly directed to persons of any age whose parents are living. In the Jewish understanding, however, the commandment was not directed primarily to young children to tell them how to treat their parents. It was directed primarily to adults, stating how mature adults were to treat their older or elderly parents. Remember *pius* Aeneas! That does not mean it is inapplicable to children. It applies to them also. But importantly, the commandment focuses on the mature person, no longer under the control of parents and now probably stronger than parents in every way. It deals with elderly parents, the weaker and needier members in the relationship. To them is honor due—to those who are feeble, senile, or of diminished capacity. And interestingly, in the Jewish mind, mothers and fathers were treated equally under this commandment.

The Effect of the Christ Event on the Commandment

The seasons of Advent and Christmas invite us to ponder our family relationships. They celebrate the time when our God, the Son of God, became man and was born into a family. It is during this time of year that we reflect annually on the enduring meaning of his birth among us and its implications in our own lives. We also reflect on the effect that the birth of Christ has on the fourth commandment. In his very flesh, after all, he began to live personally that fourth commandment that his Father had given to Moses on Mount Sinai. Jesus came not to abolish the law, but to fulfill it. And he did this precisely in his own person.

Jesus reaffirmed the Decalogue as the moral core and center of the Christian life, but he did more. By his birth, life, death, resurrection, and sending the Spirit, he enabled us to live the Ten Commandments in a new way—a uniquely Christian and transforming way—a way that the Greeks and Hebrews were unable to live. He fulfilled the biblical law by pouring the love of God, the Holy Spirit, into our very hearts.

In addition to enabling us to live the commandments by his transforming love within us, Jesus also specifically reaffirmed, personalized, and expanded the letter of the biblical law in three ways.

First, St. Luke tells us about Jesus' relationship with his parents: "He went down with them and came to Nazareth, and was obedient to them" (Lk 2:51). He practiced personally what his Father gave to Moses as one of the pillars of freedom and love for the newly liberated Israelites. He honored his parents. He obeyed them.

Second, as the Catechism teaches, "The fourth commandment reminds grown children of their *responsibilities toward their parents*. As much as they can, they must give them material and moral support in old age and in times of illness, loneliness, or distress. Jesus recalls this duty of gratitude" (CCC 2218). To this end, Jesus condemns the practice of using religious laws to fail in one's duty towards one's parents.

Jesus told the Pharisees and scribes:

> For Moses said, "Honor your father and your mother," and "Whoever curses father or mother shall die." Yet you say, "If a person says to father or mother, 'Any support you might have had from me is *qorban*'" (meaning, dedicated to God), you allow him to do nothing more for his father and mother. You nullify the word of God in favor or your tradition that you have handed on. And you do many such things. (Mk 7:10–13)

The *qorban* was money or property vowed to the Temple. Jesus specifically warned that the *qorban* offering should not be used as an excuse not to support one's mother or father. To do this would be to nullify God's word—his word to honor father and mother.

Third, the most profound effect of the Christ event on the fourth commandment can be found in the letters of St. Paul, specifically, Colossians and Ephesians. "Children, obey your parents in everything, for this is pleasing to the Lord. And fathers, do not provoke your children so they may not become discouraged" (Col 3:20–21). And to the Ephesians, Paul wrote: "Children, obey your parents [in the Lord], for this is right. 'Honor your father and mother.' This is the first commandment with a promise, 'that it may go well with you, and that you may have a long life on the earth.' Fathers, do not provoke your children to anger, but bring them up with the training and instruction of the Lord" (Eph 6:1–4).

There are three significant implications from these texts. First, there is a specific, reciprocal ethic here between parents and children. This ethic never lays a duty simply on one side. Not only does it require explicit reciprocity of obligations, but acknowledges the dignity of parents and children. Second, not only are fathers (parents) to refrain from nagging their children, they are specifically exhorted in Ephesians to teach and instruct children in the way of the Lord. This brings out what was implicit in the Jewish mentality. And third, this instruction is to be done "in the Lord," in the power of the Holy Spirit within them.

Some Practical and Pastoral Implications

Christianity becomes credible in the living witness of those who seek to live this specific commandment of love unveiled in the fourth commandment. Such credibility is revealed in the love of parents surrounding and smothering their children, and so often at the same time, in the daily struggle to help aging parents out of love. The vitality and efficacy of Christ's love within us is seen in such daily witness.

And society benefits as well. We learn, after all, that "the family is the basic unit of society. A healthy family is the prerequisite of a healthy society. The authority, stability, and loving relationships that are found in families are essential for a society that wants to sustain freedom, security, and community responsibility" (*USCCA* 383).

To this end, two family groups deserve special attention as a result of the fourth commandment—the elderly and children. Alfred McBride writes: "In 1950, people sixty-five or older made up just seven percent of the population. Now (at the beginning of this millennium) the number is twelve percent, and the fastest growing age group is eighty-five and over." These statistics have faces. They are our parents and friends. Many are the elderly poor.

The fourth commandment directs us to honor them. It is challenging, for sure. There are the challenges of failing health (with the attendant visits to doctors), the psychological challenges, the effort to balance time with elderly parents and grandparents, and time to care for your own children.

> While adult children may sometimes experience a strain between raising their own children and caring for their parents, they must do what they can to help their parents. Still, not only do adult children help their parents, but many of the elderly parents also help their adult children by their continuing love, their example, and the benefit of their life-time experience. While it is right for society to help care for the elderly, the family remains the rightful source of support. (*USCCA* 377–78)

No longer are we dependent on our parents as we were as children and teenagers. They are now dependent on us. This change in roles also breeds new challenges for elderly parents, indeed resentment, that they no longer can control their own destinies. But we know, our faith teaches us, that no human life should be denigrated because an individual has lost "commercial worth." Yes, honor your father and mother!

The second group that merits our attention is our children. In addition to the discipline and love that is so essential to raising children, the Catechism emphasizes the importance of passing on our faith to our children. "Parents have the first responsibility for the education of their children in the faith, prayer, and all the virtues" (CCC 2252). This is implicit in the Jewish understanding of the fourth commandment. Ephesians makes it crystal clear that parents have the obligation to bring their children up "with the training and instruction befitting the Lord." Corresponding to the child's duty to honor his or her parents is the reciprocal duty of the Christian parent to educate his or her children in the faith, in the family, through formal and informal instruction, and above all, by way of example.

"Through the grace of the sacrament of marriage, parents receive the responsibility and privilege of *evangelizing their children*" (CCC 2225). And this should start in a child's earliest years. It is then that the name of Jesus is first taught, that prayers can and should be taught, and that the importance and obligation of Sunday Mass must be nourished and taught by example. It is also where the seeds of a religious vocation are often planted.

> Parents, by their own faith and commitment to the Church, create an environment in their homes that is conducive to helping children begin to think about a religious vocation. They should not hesitate to invite a son or daughter to consider becoming a priest or a vowed religious. In particular, parents should always encourage and support a

child who is discerning such a call. (*USCCA*
379)

Such growth in the faith is not a one-way street.
"Children in turn contribute to the *growth in holiness* of
their parents" (*CCC* 2227).

As we contemplate *pius* Aeneas carrying his father
from burning Troy with his little son clutching his
leg, how can we not think of the relationships of love,
unfolding love, which represent the meaning of the
fourth commandment at its deepest level? While we traditionally think most about the gift of family during the
Advent and Christmas seasons, we should always give
thanks to God for our parents, living and deceased; and
for our children, if we have been so blessed as to have
them. We must also always be mindful of the Child of
Bethlehem, of the Holy Family, a family where honor
went two ways—to his parents and to him, Jesus the
Lord.

Reflect

1. What is most challenging about caring for your
   parents or other loved ones as they age? What is
   most gratifying?

2. How have you balanced the expectation
   of obedience with the need to develop
   independence in your children as they have
   grown?

3. How do you decide what consequences there
   should be for disobedience?

Pray

Heavenly Father,
you have given us the model of life
in the Holy Family of Nazareth.
Help us, O Loving Father,
to make our family another Nazareth
where love, peace and joy reign.
May it be deeply contemplative,
intensely eucharistic,
revived with joy.

Help us to stay together in joy
and sorrow in family prayer.
Teach us to see Jesus in the members of our
	families,
especially in their distressing disguise.
May the eucharistic heart of Jesus
make our hearts humble like his
and help us to carry out our family duties
in a holy way.
May we love one another
as God loves each one of us,
more and more each day,
and forgive each other's faults
as you forgive our sins.

Help us, O Loving Father,
to take whatever you give
and give whatever you take with a big
	smile.

—Blessed Mother Teresa of Calcutta

FIVE

The Fifth Commandment: Life in Need of Protection

One of my friends said to me that he was certain that he had never violated the fifth commandment, the commandment that proscribes killing. I thought to myself that he might have a different view after he reads this chapter, for this commandment proscribes more than first-degree, premeditated murder.

The fifth commandment—"You shall not kill"—is a divine institution. It is short, pithy, and concise. It is simply the directive not to kill. Stated positively, its intention is to make the world safe for life, since each and every human life is precious and unique. In the words of our late Holy Father, John Paul II, each of us is an "unrepeatable reality."

In commandments five to ten, the clear focus is on how God's children, children freed from the slavery of Egypt, were to act toward each other. The first three commandments, in contrast, were focused more on their relation with God. The fourth commandment is akin to a bridge between the two sets of commandments.

The Jewish
Understanding of the Commandment

At first glance, one wonders whether this commandment ever really took hold in the Jewish mind and heart. Even a cursory reading of the Old Testament points to the fact that warfare was a regular feature of life in ancient Israel. In fact, some wars were called "holy to the Lord," with the slaughter of an enemy ordained by God. In addition, there is a long list of crimes for which a person was liable to suffer the death penalty. Called "judicial killings," they included such crimes as murder, child sacrifice, manslaughter, incest, unchastity, adultery, witchcraft, magic, idolatry, and even breaking the Sabbath.

Regarding the breaking of the Sabbath, Exodus 31 indicates:

> The LORD said to Moses, "You must also tell the Israelites: Take care to keep my sabbaths, for that is to be the token between you and me throughout the generations, to show that it is I, the LORD, who make you holy. Therefore, you must keep the sabbath as something sacred. Whoever desecrates it shall be put to death. If anyone does work on that day, he must be rooted out of his people. Six days there are for doing work, but the seventh day is the sabbath of complete rest, sacred to the LORD. Anyone who does work on the sabbath day shall be put to death." (Ex 31:12–16)

However, there was great mercy operative in the biblical law that usually made it next to impossible to carry out the death penalty. The law was astonishingly careful to protect the rights of the guilty person. In the book of Numbers 35:6–34, one can read of the Jewish concept of the six "cities of refuge." William Barclay, that great twentieth-century Scottish Protestant preacher and theologian, writes:

> The idea was not that entrance into one of these cities gave complete and everlasting safety and asylum. The idea was that, when a man reached one of these cities, he could not be handed over to the avenging next of kin of the dead man until the whole circumstances of the killing had been investigated.

With this background, it is obvious why the specific Hebrew word for *killing* (*rasah* in the Decalogue) has been the subject of much study. It is a rare word. It is used only forty-six times in the Old Testament. It means a specific kind of killing that is prohibited—basically "unauthorized killings" or generally a killing with "malice aforethought," and not the killing that takes place through war or capital punishment.

The Catechism speaks of the murder of Cain by Abel. "God declares the wickedness of this fratricide: 'What have you done? The voice of your brother's blood is crying to me from the ground. And now you are cursed from the ground, which has opened its mouth to receive your brother's blood from your hand'" (*CCC* 2259).

Properly understood, this commandment, not unlike the others, must be seen in the context of Israel's covenant with God. That covenant spells out how free people should act with each other and the promise of "long life on the land" (Dt 4:40). Fundamentally, the proscription against this kind of killing, the willful act of taking another's life, bespeaks a deeper theology on the part of the Israelites. They understood so well the preciousness of life: that life, above all, was a gift of God, indeed a creation of God. Genesis 1:26 teaches that each of us is made in God's image and likeness. Thus, to kill a person is actually to violate God.

In his book, *The Ten Commandments and Human Rights*, Walter Harrelson states it this way:

> The point is, however, that routinely and from earliest youth the community of Israel would have been warned by its recitation of this fifth commandment that such a taking of human life was not to be routine, was not to become simply a part of the ordinary practice of administering justice. . . . More and more in the later history of Israel the commandment was safeguarded by clarification of the tests that must be met before the community could apply the death penalty to any perpetrator of a crime considered to be a capital crime.

For the Israelites, all human life was thus tied to the Creator in such a way that it was simply not the prerogative of any human being to dispose of such life except in cases where the individual human being, or the community, could claim to be acting directly on behalf of God. Since each individual Israelite was bound to the Lord in the covenant, his life lay in God's hands. God alone, who had made man in his own image, had the right to terminate life. Thus an act of murder involved an assault on God's power, the taking away of that which God had given and which God alone could give, namely life itself.

The Effect of the Christ Event on the Commandment

In the Sermon on the Mount, the Lord Jesus says: "Do not think that I have come to abolish the law or the prophets. I have come not to abolish but to fulfill" (Mt 5:17). There is perhaps no commandment that better portrays Jesus' fulfilling the biblical law than the fifth commandment, the proscription against killing. Here, the word *fulfill* takes on a whole new meaning—both deeper and more expansive.

Jesus continues:

> You have heard that it was said to your ancestors, "You shall not kill; and whoever kills will be liable to judgment." But I say to you, whoever is angry with his brother will be liable to judgment, and whoever says to his brother, "*Raqa*," will be answerable to the Sanhedrin, and whoever says, "You fool," will be liable to fiery Gehenna. Therefore, if you bring your gift to the altar, and there recall that your brother has anything against you, leave your gift there at the altar, go first and be reconciled with your brother, and then come and offer your gift. Settle with your opponent quickly while on the way to court with him. (Mt 5:21–25)

In this passage from the Sermon on the Mount, Matthew seeks to teach precisely how Jesus himself fulfills the law and the prophets. "You have heard it said . . . but I say." Jesus deepens, interiorizes, radicalizes, specifies, clarifies, and concretizes the law. Not only is murder or unauthorized killing proscribed, but Jesus asserts that growing angry, using abusive language, and holding of anyone in contempt are likewise against this commandment. His words are an intensification of the force of the fifth commandment.

Jesus directs his message to one's interior disposition—growing angry (that profound lack of love)—which can result in killing, in harming another. Misplaced and inappropriate anger in itself can kill even the best of friendships. It is hard to give up anger. Certainly it can shatter any semblance of civility in a family, in a marital relationship, between an attorney and client, a doctor and patient, and in the workplace at all levels. Of course, Jesus' focus on one's interior disposition (anger) in no way seeks to relativize the concrete evil of killing.

By underscoring the evil of anger and abusive speech, Jesus seeks to turn something external into something internal without in any way abandoning the external precept. In effect, Jesus demands more than refraining from murder. He desires love and mercy. This requires each of us to come to terms with the power of God within us, the new life of the Holy Spirit, the life made possible by the death and resurrection of Jesus. He pours God's life within us, a love that can transform us and help open our hearts, a love that dissipates all anger. Not only does Jesus proscribe anger, he makes it possible by his very life within us to live without anger.

This life, his life, is powerful indeed. It is our coopera-
tion, our yielding to the Holy Spirit that allows him con-
tinually to overpower us and free us ever anew. Love
makes the world safe for life.

Regarding this love, Alfred McBride writes:

> So long as love is experienced and practiced,
> life has a chance: This is the basic message of
> the Fifth Commandment. If this value were
> absorbed into our inner lives it would crowd
> out the destructive impulses that beget anti-
> life behavior. This liberating value of the
> Fifth Commandment would free us from
> war, murder, genocide, terrorism, abortion
> and all the other forms of mayhem humans
> inflict on one another.
>
> Love is the closest experience we have to the
> act of creation. Love does not murder life.
> Love wants to produce, sustain and care for
> it. Some speak of love as a seamless garment
> that wraps its creative protectiveness around
> life from conception to death.

Love is thus the central, greatest, and primary
commandment. It is the "fulfillment of the law" (Rom
13:8–10).

In the Sermon on the Mount, Jesus amplifies even
further the requirements of the fifth commandment.
He speaks of the need for reconciliation, the urgency of
reconciliation, of being reconciled brothers and sisters.
"Therefore, if you bring your gift to the altar, and there
recall that your brother has anything against you, leave
your gift there at the altar, go first and be reconciled

with your brother, and then come and offer your gift" (Mt 5:24). Not enough is heard today of reconciliation in families, reconciliation between nations, and above all reconciliation with God. Conversely, we seem to dwell on dysfunction, even as a justification for certain destructive conduct. And yet central to the Church's mission, the mission of each and every member of the Church, is the reconciliation among peoples. It is so linked to the conversion of hearts, a daily challenge for each of us.

In the Sermon on the Mount, Jesus even goes so far as to make the task of reconciliation a part of fulfillment of the fifth commandment. No friendship, no relationship need fail forever. The healing and restorative grace that only Christ can give in that great healing sacrament of Penance is indispensable for reconciliation. It should be a regular part of our walk with the Lord. It certainly will help us in our efforts to live fully the fifth commandment.

Some Practical and Pastoral Implications

The Catechism speaks of three areas that come under the fifth commandment—respect for human life, respect for the dignity of persons, and safeguarding peace. Each of us must reflect on these areas and see if our actions or omissions make us offenders against the fifth commandment. There are practical implications for us.

Respect for Human Life

The Vatican Congregation for the Doctrine of the Faith, on September 8, 2008, issued an important document entitled *The Dignity of a Person (Dignitas Personae)*. Two fundamental principles draw from *The Gift of Life (Donum Vitae)*, a 1987 document in this same area, and are set forth to help us understand the Church's teaching on human life and procreation. The first principle treats human life and its origin. It states that the human embryo,

> . . . the fruit of human generation, from the first moment of its existence, that is to say, from the moment the zygote has formed, demands the unconditional respect that is morally due to the human being in his bodily and spiritual totality. The human being is to be respected and treated as a person from the moment of conception; and therefore from the same moment his rights as a person must be recognized, among which in the first place is the inviolable right of every innocent human being to life. (*DP* 4, 2)

The second principle treats procreation and states:

> The origin of human life has its authentic context in marriage and in the family, where it is generated through an act which expresses the reciprocal love between a man and a woman. Procreation which is truly responsible vis-à-vis the child to be born must be the fruit of marriage. (*DP* 6)

With those two principles in mind, the Catechism teaches that "God alone is the Lord of life from its beginning until its end: no one can under any circumstance claim for himself the right directly to destroy an innocent human being" (*CCC* 2258). One would otherwise be in violation of the fifth commandment. Here are six concrete examples where the violation of the fifth commandment takes place:

1. *Abortion.* Since *Roe v. Wade* in 1973, the Supreme Court decision that declared abortion to be a matter of Constitutional right, there have been over fifty million abortions in the United States, young children dying before they had the opportunity to enjoy life outside the womb. From earliest Christianity, "the *Didache (The Teaching of the Apostles)*, 2,2, written toward the end of the first century and revered as an honored guide for Christian life, we read, 'You shall not kill the embryo by abortion.' This teaching has never changed and it will not change" (*USCCA* 391).

    Our church is always and will always be on the side of life—from conception until natural death. This is both a theological issue and a moral issue, an issue that has regrettably become political. It is precisely because Jesus took on life, took on our human flesh and ennobled it by becoming man, that we value human life.

    The pro-life movement, in effect, was born at Christmas for, as a result of Jesus' birth, our human life takes on new value. "For, by his incarnation, he, the Son of God, has in a certain way united himself with each man. He worked with human hands, he thought with a human mind. He acted with a human will, and with a human heart, he loved" (*GS* 22). By embracing our human condition in everything but sin, Jesus revealed the dignity and the surpassing worth of the human condition. He thus linked himself to us forever, to each one of us, by taking on our human flesh. He gives ultimate meaning to the human condition in all its brokenness by his own birth in a manger. The mystery of Christmas, of what happened on that cold Bethlehem night, is precisely why the Church consistently and untiringly advocates the protection of all human life from conception to natural death. The Church will never abandon the human person, especially the suffering human person, because each of us is so closely and unbreakably linked with Christ, with the mystery of Christmas, with the eternal meaning he gave and continues to give each of us by making his dwelling among us.

2. *Human embryos produced by in vitro fertilization.* In this process, the conjugal act is bypassed and "spare embryos" are routinely created and destroyed. Thus both the method of procuring embryos—by avoiding the conjugal act—and the resulting destruction of unused embryos render in vitro fertilization immoral.

3. *The state taking the life of a guilty person by the death penalty (except in rare cases).* Quoting the late Pope John Paul II, the Catechism clearly reads:

> Today, in fact, as a consequence of the possibilities which the state has for effectively preventing crime, by rendering one who has committed an offense incapable of doing harm—without definitively taking away from him the possibility of redeeming himself—the cases in which the execution of the offender is an absolute necessity "are very rare, if not practically non-existent" (CCC 2267).

4. *Euthanasia or assisted suicide.* This is the direct killing of a person or the assisting of a person to kill himself or herself. "Intentional euthanasia, sometimes called mercy killing, is murder. Regardless of the motives or means, euthanasia consists of putting to death those who are sick, are disabled, or are dying" (*USCCA* 393). The Church's opposition to euthanasia does not mean that extraordinary efforts must be undertaken to keep people alive, however. "Catholic moral tradition has always taught that we can discontinue medical procedures that are burdensome, extraordinary, and disproportionate to the outcome" (*USCCA* 394).

5. *The use of human stem cells for research.* Some scientists look to the human embryo as the best source for stem cells. "The moral problem is that in order to retrieve the stem cells, the growing child must be killed. But every embryo from the moment of conception has the entire genetic makeup of a unique human life. The growing child must be recognized and treated as completely and fully human. He or she needs only time to grow and develop. To destroy an embryo is to take a human life, an act contrary to God's law and Church teaching" (*USCCA* 392). On the other hand, the use of adult stem cells is permissible. "Stem cells from placenta, bone marrow, and the umbilical cord are being used to treat leukemia. This is a promising field of research that does not involve the moral implications of embryonic stem cell research" (*USCCA* 393).

6. *Suicide.* The willful taking of one's own life is a grievous sin and violates the fifth commandment. After all: "It is God who remains the sovereign Master of life" (*CCC* 2280). At the same time, the

Church prays for those who have taken their own lives, and we should not despair of their eternal salvation. "By ways known to him alone, God can provide the opportunity for salutary repentance" (*CCC* 2283).

In all of these situations, it is important to underscore that just because something may be legally protected or even permissible, that does not necessarily confer a moral right to exercise the legal right in question.

Respect for the Dignity of Persons

Respect for the dignity of the person stems from the fact that we were made in the image and likeness of God. This section of the Catechism includes many moral issues that we might not immediately associate with the proscription against killing (*CCC* 2284–2301). As an example, we are taught to avoid scandalizing people. "Scandal is a grave offense when by deed or omission it deliberately leads others to sin gravely" (*CCC* 2284). We are also taught to take good care of our health. "Life and physical health are precious gifts entrusted to us by God" (*CCC* 2288). "The virtue of temperance disposes us to avoid every kind of excess: the abuse of food, alcohol, tobacco or medicine" (*CCC* 2290). The fifth commandment also forbids bigotry and hatred, physical and emotional abuse, and violence of any kind against another person.

Safeguarding Peace

"Blessed are the peacemakers, for they shall be called children of God" (Mt 5:9). In the Beatitudes, the Lord teaches us to be peacemakers. The eight Beatitudes are not optional if we are to follow the Lord. They form the Magna Carta of the Christian moral life. In the upper room after the resurrection, the risen Lord twice says to his disciples, "Peace be with you." He gives us his kind of peace, a peace that the world can never give.

Each January 1, the World Day of Prayer for Peace, our Holy Father helps form the conscience of the world by insisting that peace is possible and that it is our duty to teach peace and work for peace and pray for peace. "Because of the evils and injustices that accompany all war, the Church insistently urges everyone to prayer and to action so that the divine Goodness may free us from the ancient bondage of war" (CCC 2307). The Catechism is clear on the principles of legitimate defense and the possibility of a just war.

In each of the above three areas, we are called to see the underlying presence of the fifth commandment, the commandment not to kill. It is our perennial challenge to make God's law, the law enshrined in this and every commandment, a vital part of our lives and of the lives of those with whom we live, work, and play.

At first glance, the friend I mentioned at the beginning of this chapter, who said that he had never violated the fifth commandment, might be right. Most probably, he is! But the fifth commandment, as we have seen, is much broader than it might seem at first glance. I hope this chapter has helped make that clear.

Reflect

1. What is something that you are doing or could do to demonstrate your respect for the sacredness of life?

2. How can you as an individual help to break the growing cycle of violence in our society?

3. How might your daily interaction with co-workers, neighbors, family members, service clerks, etc., better reflect your respect for life?

Pray

Heavenly Father,
the beauty and dignity of human life
was the crowning of your creation.
You further ennobled that life
when your Son became one with us in his
   incarnation.
Help us to realize the sacredness of human
   life
and to respect it from the moment of
   conception
until the last moment at death.
Give us courage to speak with truth and
   love,
and with conviction in defense of life.

Help us to extend the gentle hand of mercy
   and forgiveness
to those who do not reverence your gift of
   life.

To all, grant pardon for the times we have
    failed
to be grateful for your precious gift of life
or to respect it in others.
We ask this in Jesus' name. Amen.

—Catholic Doors Ministry

SIX

The Sixth Commandment:
Sex, Marriage, and
Purity of Heart

T he sixth commandment, "You shall not commit
adultery," is stated in the same words in both
Exodus 20:14 and Deuteronomy 5:18. As with
the fifth commandment, there is more to the sixth commandment than meets the eye. The Catechism teaches:
"The tradition of the Church has understood the sixth
commandment as encompassing the whole of human
sexuality" (*CCC* 2336).

The Jewish
Understanding of the Commandment

Like the fifth commandment, this commandment is
extremely terse, short, and concise. Unlike the fifth commandment, where the word *kill* is open to various inter-
pretations, the Hebrew word for adultery, *n'p*, is not.
There are no major linguistic problems, and the word
is less ambiguous. There is a specific understanding,
moreover, of what adultery meant for the people of the
Old Testament times.

In his commentary on Deuteronomy, Patrick Miller
states:

> In the Old Testament, this commandment meant that the wife was prohibited from sexual intercourse with any other male (other than her husband) and the husband from sexual intercourse with any other married woman. A man could have intercourse with a concubine or a prostitute without coming under the sanction of this commandment.

In the Jewish mentality, adultery is thus specifically and uniquely the crime against the marriage bed rather than sexual irregularity in general.

As in the case of killing, the law against adultery simply states the prohibition and does so in a seemingly unqualified way. Paradoxically, there seems to have been no sin that was regarded in Judaism with greater horror than adultery. At the same time, there was no sin, to judge by the rebuke of the sages and prophets, that was more common.

William Barclay comments:

> "He who commits adultery," said the Sage, "has no sense; he who does it destroys himself" (Proverbs 6:32). . . . There are three who never return from Gehenna—the adulterer, he who puts his fellowman to shame in public, and he who calls his fellowman by an opprobrious nickname. . . . Destruction will come upon them, "because they have committed folly in Israel, they have committed adultery with their neighbours' wives" (Jeremiah 29:23). Ezekiel flings his accusation against the nation in his day: "Adulterous wife, who receives

strangers instead of her husband!" (Ezekiel 16:32). "And I will judge you as women who break wedlock and shed blood are judged" (Ezekiel 16:38).

From the prophet Hosea we hear: "Yes, their mother has played the harlot; she that conceived them has acted shamefully" (Hos 2:7). Deuteronomy tells us that a man or woman caught in adultery was subject to death—both of them—an indication of how serious this sin was considered. "Thus shall you purge evil from your midst" (Dt 22:22).

While adultery is often mentioned in the Old Testament, only in 2 Samuel 11–12, the well-known account of the adulterous King David and Bathsheba, is the crime described in detail. Only after an adulterous relationship with Bathsheba, before the birth of their child, and after David had her legitimate husband killed in battle to conceal the original crime, did David finally repent. The Lord spoke to him through Nathan, who said: "'The LORD on his part has forgiven your sin: you shall not die. But since you have utterly spurned the LORD by this deed, the child born to you must surely die'" (2 Sam 12:13–14).

Yes, there was the compassion of God for David! But David had to live with the consequences of his act—and so do we. David Noel Freedman, professor of history, explains it this way:

> For the author/editor of Samuel, David's adultery with Bathsheba was a turning point not only in David's reign, but in the history of the kingdom. All the subsequent trials and ills of the later years, the rebellions

and machinations, are described as stemming from that violation by the king, who compounded adultery with murder, forfeited the respect and loyalty of his troops and thus distanced himself from Yahweh, the covenant and the privileged status he enjoyed as the anointed of Yahweh.

This language of covenant gets us to the heart of the matter. As Alfred McBride so beautifully describes:

> The primary concern of the Sixth Commandment is not adultery so much as fidelity. In fact, no other commandment so fundamentally reflects the covenant, the basis of the commandments, as does the covenant fidelity of husband and wife illumined by this sixth invitation from God. . . . In the Hebrew covenant, marriage was meant to reflect the wedding between God and Israel with irresistible affection. . . . Such fidelity implies more than abstention from adultery; it rejoices in the challenge to be faithful.

The challenge to be faithful! For the Jewish mind, this was at the heart of the proscription against adultery. The commandment parallels the first commandment against having other gods. Both portray a clear act of unfaithfulness that is reprehensible to the God of the covenant, whose character it is to be totally faithful. It is faithfulness expressed in loving obedience. And it permeates every sphere of life, both religious and secular. This is the way free people live. This gives a distinctive character to the biblical law on adultery. Adultery committed by one partner in a marriage involved not only unfaithfulness to the other partner, but also unfaithfulness to God.

The essential value involved here is the protection of the sanctity of the marriage relationship—that covenant of a man and a woman freely entered into for life. As we learn from Genesis: "That is why a man leaves his father and mother and clings to his wife, and the two of them become one body" (Gn 2:24). This is the monogamous ideal of marriage. And adultery, taken very seriously, assuredly undercuts and damages this sacred relationship and undercuts the covenant with the God of Israel.

In addition, the biblical law, the law given by God, was clearly countercultural. It stood in some tension with the practices of the time: the legality of polygamy, the toleration of prostitution, the practices of the surrounding Canaanite neighbors, and the linkage of prostitution with the religious cult of such Canaanite deities as Baal. In sum, chastity, particularly in the context of marriage, was held at high value under the biblical law. The sixth commandment sought to protect it. And in a world replete with pagan-temple prostitutes, the biblical law stood squarely on the side of monogamy and faithfulness. In practice, monogamy and faithfulness more and more prevailed. The strictness of the law was rooted in the sanctity of the institution being protected.

The Effect of the Christ Event on the Commandment

There are two ways in which the Christ event deepened the Jewish understanding of the proscription against adultery. The Catechism teaches: "Jesus came to restore creation to the purity of its origins" (CCC 2336). How did he do this?

First, we look once again at the Sermon on the Mount in the Gospel of St. Matthew, where our Lord interprets God's plan strictly. He teaches: "You have heard that it was said, 'You shall not commit adultery.' But I say to you, everyone who looks at a woman with lust has already committed adultery with her in his heart" (Mt 5:27–28).

Not only the act of adultery but the lustful thought is proscribed by Jesus. The teaching of Jesus thus turns the sixth commandment on its head. He turns something external into something internal without abandoning the external precept. Jesus demands more than the absence of adultery. He even proscribes looking lustfully at a woman.

And he gives us the Holy Spirit, the Spirit of his abiding, ever-faithful love, to help us, to renew our minds, to make us pure in thought, word, and deed. We are exhorted by St. Paul in his Letter to the Romans: "Do not conform yourself to this age but be transformed by the renewal of your mind, that you may discern what is the will of God, what is good and pleasing and perfect" (Rom 12:2). This is the work of the Holy Spirit.

In the face of temptation, we must yield to the movement of the Holy Spirit that our minds might be renewed. Our minds are often described as the factories of sin. Our bodies are meant, however, to be temples of the Holy Spirit, the living God within us, renewing us, molding us into his loving image—his heart and mind. That is the great benefit of being reborn of water and the Holy Spirit, of being a member of his body, the Church.

You might ask what it means to look at someone lustfully. In effect, it means reducing the other person to an object with a look. This look is a way of gratifying one's own physical desires without giving of oneself to that person—a gift which would be present if there were a genuine "communion of persons." This look thus violates the infinite dignity of both persons. In the case of a spouse, when lust dominates, it is not possible to express a mutual, selfless, and freely given gift to the other person. Selfishness is not a selfless gift of love.

There is another significant way that Jesus transformed and deepened the Jewish understanding of adultery. Listen again to St. Matthew's Gospel:

> Some Pharisees approached him, and tested him, saying, "Is it lawful for a man to divorce his wife for any cause whatever?" He said in reply, "Have you not read that from the beginning the Creator 'made them male and female' and said, 'For this reason a man shall leave his father and mother and be joined to his wife, and the two shall become one flesh'? So they are no longer two, but one flesh. Therefore, what God has joined together, no human being must separate." They said to him, "Then why did Moses command that the man give the woman a bill of divorce and dismiss [her]?" He said to them, "Because of the hardness of your hearts Moses allowed you to divorce your wives, but from the beginning it was not so. I say to you, whoever divorces his wife (unless the marriage is unlawful) and marries another commits adultery." (Mt 19:3–10)

In addition to appearing in the text of St. Matthew, this teaching of Jesus regarding adultery is found in Mark 10:2–12 and Luke 16:18. The teaching against divorce is found in 1 Corinthians 7:10.

Divorce and remarriage were permitted by Moses, but not encouraged. With the coming of Jesus, however, divorce and remarriage were forbidden. In fact, such behavior was seen as a form of adultery. The exemptive clause in Matthew, "unless the marriage is unlawful," seems to refer to an incestuous union within forbidden degrees of kinship. Such a union would not be a true marriage anyway. The Catechism teaches: "the sixth commandment and the New Testament forbid adultery absolutely" (CCC 2380).

Jesus uses as the basis of his teaching the language of Genesis that reads "from the beginning [of creation]" a man leaves father and mother and is joined to his wife and the "two shall become one flesh." Indissoluble— forever one! Short of that, adultery takes place—another radical spin placed by Jesus on the law of Moses. This firms up the sanctity of marriage and the permanence of the marriage covenant.

It is important to understand that what is forbidden by the Catholic Church, following the teaching of Jesus, is divorce and remarriage, for one cannot be married to more than one spouse at the same time. An ecclesiastical declaration of *nullity* (annulment), which the Church requires for one who has received a civil divorce and hopes to marry in the Church, is a judgment by a Church tribunal that the prior union was never a valid marriage from the beginning. A finding of nullity means that the person is free to marry in the Church and would not thereby commit the adultery prohibited by God's law. We should all encourage and support a person who finds him or herself in the often traumatic and very difficult situation of a divorce, and encourage that person to consider exploring the possibility of an annulment if he or she contemplates a future marriage. It is hoped that this process would further healing and reconciliation.

In addition to healing and reconciliation, we continue to see the compassionate face of Jesus in his revealed Word. We see it, for example, in his forgiveness of the adulterous woman, a woman who could have been stoned to death according to the law of Moses. It is truly and importantly the effect of the Christ event on this commandment. John's Gospel tells us:

> [Jesus] bent down and began to write on the ground with his finger. But when they continued asking him, he straightened up and said to them, "Let the one among you who is without sin be the first to throw a stone at her." Again he bent down and wrote on the ground. And in response, they went away one by one, beginning with the elders. So he was left alone with the woman before him. Then Jesus straightened up and said to her, "Woman, where are they? Has no one condemned you?" She replied, "No one, sir." Then Jesus said, "Neither do I condemn you. Go, (and) from now on do not sin any more." (Jn 8:6–11)

Some Practical and Pastoral Implications

Two areas have concrete pastoral and practical implications for the living out of the sixth commandment. They include the vocation to chastity and marriage itself.

First, under the section of the sixth commandment, the Catechism has a whole treatment on the vocation to chastity—that successful integration of sexuality within the person, and thus "the inner unity of man in his bodily and spiritual being" (*CCC* 2337). Most of us have never quite thought that each one of us, without exception, has this vocation to chastity regardless of our state in life. "All people—married, single, religious and ordained—need to acquire the virtue of chastity" (*USCCA* 405).

> Chastity unites our sexuality with our entire human nature. It approaches sexuality as related to our spiritual natures so that sex is seen as more than a physical act. Sexuality affects the whole person because of the unity of body and soul. Jesus is the model of chastity. "Chastity includes an *apprenticeship in self-mastery* which is a training in human freedom" (*CCC* 2339). The acquisition of chastity depends on self-discipline and leads to an internal freedom, which enables human beings to temper sexual desires according to God's plan for the appropriate expression of love in the marital relationship of a man and a woman." (*USCCA* 405)

More effort must be expended on our human development, beginning in the family. As followers of Jesus, we acquire chastity through the long and exacting work of self-mastery. It begins during childhood and continues through adolescence and adulthood. It is supported by the grace and gift of the Holy Spirit within us that helps us to live virtuous lives (and thus imitate the purity of Christ). Ultimately, this virtue of chastity blossoms into friendships with one's neighbor.

I asked my parish RCIA group to describe some of the values that help define true friendships. Regrettably, true and chaste friendships are so often a lost art in our day. They responded by highlighting the importance of loyalty among friends, openness and honesty, the exchanging of advice, and attempts at genuine mutual understanding. They also mentioned the sharing of activities and even hardships with each other and being pro-active with one another. Chastity in friendships is thus possible and to be encouraged!

At the same time, the Catechism lists the following as offenses against chastity: lust, masturbation, fornication, pornography, prostitution, rape, and homosexual acts (*CCC* 2351–2357). Apropos of the final item, the *United States Catholic Catechism for Adults* makes it clear that "having homosexual inclinations is not immoral. It is homosexual acts that are immoral" (*USCCA* 407).

Second, it is important to add a word about marriage when writing about the sixth commandment! Marriage has a specific meaning. By definition, first and foremost, God is the author of marriage. This institution created by God involves a faithful, exclusive, and lifelong union between a man and a woman. We know this from the order of nature, the light of human reason, and confirmation by divine revelation found in scripture. Any other proposed definition of marriage, even one enshrined in legislation, is not marriage.

The Catechism lists the following as threats to marriage: adultery, divorce, cohabitation (an unmarried couple living together), polygamy, and attempts to justify same-sex unions giving them matrimonial status (cf. *USCCA* 410–411).

The Vatican document *Dignity of a Person*, teaches:

> Marriage, present in all times and in all cultures, "is in reality something wisely and providently instituted by God the Creator with a view to carrying out his loving plan in human beings. Thus husband and wife, through the reciprocal gift of themselves to the other—something which is proper and exclusive to them—bring about that communion of persons by which they perfect each other, so as to cooperate with God in the procreation and raising of new lives." In the fruitfulness of married love, man and woman "make it clear that at the origin of their spousal life there is a genuine 'yes,' which is pronounced and truly lived in reciprocity, remaining ever open to life." (*DP* 6)

"The bond between husband and wife is both conjugal and procreative. Conjugal mutual love and fidelity is the *unitive* aspect of marriage. The *procreative* aspect of marriage concerns the conception, birth, and education of children. The bond between the unitive and procreative may not be broken" (*USCCA* 408). The Catechism clearly teaches that "these two meanings or values of marriage cannot be separated without altering the couple's spiritual life and compromising the goods of marriage and future of the family" (CCC 2363). Both are essential for a proper understanding of marriage itself. So important is the openness to children as an integral part of marriage that the Church teaches consistently that "'it is necessary that each and every marriage act remain ordered *per se* to the procreation of human life'" (CCC 2366).

"The origin of human life has its authentic context in marriage and in the family, where it is generated through an act which expresses the reciprocal love between a man and a woman. Procreation which is truly responsible vis-à-vis the child to be born must be the fruit of marriage" (*DP* 6). Efforts to achieve pregnancy outside of the act of sexual intercourse (e.g., by in vitro fertilization) are thus morally wrong, as is artificial contraception where openness to life is artificially restricted.

Cardinal Caffarra, the Archbishop of Bologna, writes perceptively, "This truth (regarding the inseparability of the unitive from the procreative) is substantially reducible to the affirmation that every act of sexual union carries indelibly inscribed within itself the sense of being both a gift of total, definitive and faithful love and an act intrinsically ordered to the co-creation of human life."

The Church also makes it clear that "periodic continence, that is, the methods of birth regulation based on self-observation and the use of infertile periods, is in conformity with the objective criteria of morality" (CCC 2370).

I conclude this chapter with a word of respect and encouragement for those of you who are living a life of faithfulness and chastity both in the single and married state. Your witness reminds each of us ever anew that with proper understanding and God's faithful love, the sixth commandment, as challenging as it can be, continues to be a powerful sign of God's love for us and our families in this world of ours.

Reflect

1. How do you deal with the pressures of society to view sex only as a source of pleasure or entertainment?

2. In your experience, what are the reasons for the success of marriages that endure for a lifetime?

3. How have healthy relationships with others contributed to your spirituality?

Pray

Gratitude for Gift of Sexuality

Loving God, source of all truth and strength, help me to come to know you more fully through a greater awareness of myself and those closest to me.

I know that through loving others I can come to a greater awareness of your presence by entering into the challenges and joys of a healthy relationship. Be with me as I strive to be open to your great mystery in my life and in the lives of those I love.

As I try to understand the great gift of my sexuality, help me to be true to what is deepest in my heart. Give me the patience to be still and listen for your voice in the depths of my being.

Then, help me to express this gift, with all of its mystery, in accord with what is true within me. Grant me the strength to resist the pressures from others when it is not in keeping with your will for me.

May my need for emotional intimacy not over-shadow an honest decision about what I want to say physically. I know that in choosing to remain true to myself, I am also being truthful to you and those I love so dearly.

Gracious God, be with me in times of doubt. Help me to express my true giftedness in all of my choices and actions.

—Darrell R. Paulsen

SEVEN

The Seventh Commandment: Don't Steal—Act with Justice and Love

The seventh commandment, stated simply, is "You shall not steal." It is the third in a trilogy of commandments that are terse and direct and lack an explicit object. The prohibition against theft is akin to the prohibition against murder and adultery.

The Church has greatly amplified its understanding of this commandment to include respect for the property of others, the demands of justice and charity with respect to others (i.e., the social teaching of the Church), and the call to be faithful stewards of the goods of creation.

> To keep this Commandment, we need to acquire the virtues of moderation in our possessions, justice in our treatment of others, respect for their human dignity, and solidarity with all peoples. Moderation curbs our attachments to worldly goods and restrains our appetite for consumerism. Justice helps us respect our neighbor's rights and be interested in their human well-being. Solidarity opens our hearts to identifying

with the whole human family, reminding us
of our common humanity. (*USCCA* 419)

The Jewish
Understanding of the Commandment

At first glance, the commandment seems to be a simple prohibition against theft, i.e., the unlawful acquisi-
tion of the property and possessions of another person
or group of persons. After all, simple theft was forbidden under biblical law, and restitution was required.

In Exodus, we read:

> If a thief is caught in the act of housebreaking
> and beaten to death, there is no bloodguilt
> involved. But if after sunrise he is thus
> beaten, there is bloodguilt. He must make full
> restitution. If he has nothing, he shall be sold
> to pay for his theft. If what he stole is found
> alive in his possession, be it an ox, an ass or
> a sheep, he shall restore two animals for each
> one stolen. When a man is burning over a
> field or a vineyard, if he lets the fire spread so
> that it burns in another's field, he must make
> restitution with the best produce of his own
> field or vineyard. . . . When a man gives money
> or an article to another for safekeeping and it
> is stolen from the latter's house, the thief, if
> caught, must make twofold restitution. (Ex
> 22:1–6)

As in parts of the developing world today, most
people in Old Testament times had few belongings.

Unlawful theft could be devastating for their survival. Hence, restitution was an essential penalty. Generally, a thief had to pay twice the value and sometimes up to five times the value of the item stolen.

Upon closer scrutiny, however, it appears that the strictures of the seventh commandment, in the Jewish mind and understanding, were more specific. At least originally, theft was concerned not with property but specifically with relationships among people within the covenant community. The primary thrust of the commandment is against "man stealing," which is akin to kidnapping. In effect, it is a ban against enslavement. Deuteronomy states that "if any man is caught kidnapping a fellow Israelite in order to enslave him and sell him, the kidnapper shall be put to death" (Dt 24:7, cf. Ex 21:16). Like the commandments against murder and adultery, kidnapping was a capital crime, and the penalty was death.

The best example of this kind of crime is found in Genesis 37:19–36. This passage deals with the seizure and sale of Joseph by his brothers to traveling Midianite traders. Genesis 40:15 describes him as "kidnapped from the land of the Hebrews." He became a slave in Egypt. The essential wrongness of this kind of "personal" theft is its enslaving quality—the complete dominion or manipulation of one human being by another. Similar to the second commandment—the prohibition against taking the Lord's name in vain (the improper use of God's name or manipulating God for one's personal use)—the seventh commandment prohibition against man stealing is meant to stop the manipulation of others for personal gain.

This commandment must always be seen within the covenant context. It prohibited the attempted domination or manipulation of God or a fellow Israelite, which would cause a disruption of the relationship between a person and the community. One can understand theft seen initially (originally) in this light. After all, the Israelites never forgot they were descendants of slaves themselves. The seventh commandment, understood at least initially as a prohibition against slavery, was a permanent reminder of their enslavement, a reminder given them by God himself.

In time, the form of the commandment and the Jewish understanding of it became more inclusive and the application broader, prohibiting property theft as well as the theft of human beings. The Hebrew verb for *steal* began to be used with things or property as its object, in addition to persons. Note, however, that the same concerns undergirded the seventh commandment, even as its reach broadened, i.e., manipulation, disruption, domination, enslavement, and exploitation. Substantial domination is possible by controlling another's property as well as by controlling another's person.

Witness David's appropriate rage at hearing Nathan's story of the rich person's taking the single lamb from a poor man to avoid using his own. "David grew very angry with that man and said to Nathan: 'As the Lord lives, the man who has done this merits death! He shall restore the ewe lamb fourfold because he has done this and has had no pity'" (2 Sam 12:5–6). The theft of a single lamb was tantamount to stealing the poor man himself. It was in effect theft of all he had.

The safeguard on property thus protects, for each person, a sphere of moral self-supervision and self-determination against the threat of enslavement or exploitation. The common reaction of persons who are victims of theft of property in their homes is a strong sense of having been personally violated. Both the joy and danger of having personal property is that it represents, to some extent, an extension of self. At base, it is this understanding that the seventh commandment seeks to promote.

The Effect of the Christ Event on the Commandment

In all three of the synoptic gospels, within the context of the story of the rich young man, Jesus makes the seventh commandment proscription against theft his own. "You shall not steal" is thus a part of Christ's teaching also (cf. Mt 19:18, Mk 10:19, Lk 18:20). From the Zacchaeus story, we know that restitution is also a part of Christ's teaching. Jesus blesses Zacchaeus for his pledge: "If I have extorted anything from anyone I shall repay it four times over" (Lk 19:8).

As if to highlight this proscription, St. Paul adds further that neither "thieves nor the greedy nor drunkards nor slanderers nor robbers will inherit the kingdom of God" (1 Cor 6:10). In Matthew, underscoring the need for vigilance against thieves, Jesus tells the parable about the thief in the night, saying, "If the master of the house had known the hour of night, when the thief was coming, he would have stayed awake and not let his house be broken into" (Mt 24:43). Finally, in contrast to the thieves and robbers who have come to steal the sheep, Jesus says: "A thief comes only to steal and slaughter and destroy; I came that they might have life and have it more abundantly" (Jn 10:10). It is Jesus who gives us life by his ever-abiding grace in contrast to the thief, who like sin, conveys death and enslavement.

Perhaps the most lasting effect of the Christ event regarding the seventh commandment concerns the whole question of property—so often the object of theft—and its relationship to the dignity of the human person. Reflect on the story of the rich young man with this in mind.

> Now someone approached him and said, "Teacher, what good must I do to gain eternal life?" He answered him, "Why do you ask me about the good? There is only One who is good. If you wish to enter into life, keep the commandments." He asked him, "Which ones?" And Jesus replied, "You shall not kill; you shall not commit adultery; you shall not steal; you shall not bear false witness; honor your father and your mother;" and "you shall love your neighbor as yourself. " The young man said to him, "All of these I have observed. What do I still lack?" Jesus said to him, "If you wish to be perfect, go, sell what you have and give to [the] poor, and you will have treasure in heaven. Then come, follow me." When the young man heard this statement, he went away sad, for he had many possessions. (Mt 19:16–22)

What is Jesus telling us about private property, our possessions? William Barclay's comments are insightful:

> Here . . . is the point. Private property is not in the least wrong, when the owner of

> it remembers that he possesses it, not only to use it for himself, but also to use it for others. But private property is a kind of theft when a man uses it for nothing but his own pleasure and his own gratification, with never a thought for anyone else. It is not the property but the selfishness which constitutes the theft.

The misuse of our property is theft and a violation of the seventh commandment. As with the other commandments, Jesus goes beyond the strict letter of the law, despite the importance of its face value for him. He teaches the value of detachment—selfless detachment from material goods—and urges that these be sacrificed for higher spiritual goods. For some, this even meant abandoning their livelihood to follow him. "At once they left their nets and followed him" (Mt 4:20).

As followers of Jesus, we are exhorted to seek first the kingdom of God:

> Do not store up for yourselves treasures on earth, where moth and decay destroy, and thieves break in and steal. But store up treasures in heaven, where neither moth nor decay can destroy, nor thieves break in and steal. For where your treasure is, there also will your heart be. (Mt 6:19–21)

This teaching helps us understand, after all, that the goods of creation belong to the whole human race. "In the beginning God entrusted the earth and its resources to the common stewardship of mankind to take care of them, master them by labor, and enjoy their fruits" (CCC 2402).

Jesus' admonition not "to lay up for yourselves an earthly treasure," and his counsel to the rich young man, and to each of us, to sell his and our possessions and give to the poor does not undercut the Church's consistent teaching regarding the right to private property and its important relationship to the development of the human person. The Catechism teaches: "The ownership of any property makes its holder a steward of Providence, with the task of making it fruitful and communicating its benefits to others, first of all his family" (CCC 2404).

Our late Holy Father John Paul II wrote in *On the Hundredth Anniversary (Centesimus Annus)*, one of his major social encyclicals:

> In *Rerum Novarum*, Leo XIII strongly affirmed the natural character of the right to private property, using various arguments against the socialism of his time. This right, which is fundamental for the autonomy and development of the person, has always been defended by the Church up to our own day. At the same time, the Church teaches that the possession of material goods is not an absolute right, and that its limits are inscribed in its very nature as a human right.

> While the Pope proclaimed the right to private ownership, he affirmed with equal clarity that the "use" of goods, while marked by freedom, is subordinated to their original common destination as created goods, as well as to the will of Jesus Christ as expressed in the Gospel. Pope Leo wrote: "Those whom

fortune favors are admonished . . . that they should tremble at the warnings of Jesus Christ . . . and that a most strict account must be given to the Supreme Judge for the use of all they possess"; and quoting Saint Thomas Aquinas, he added: "But if the question be asked, how must one's possessions be used? the Church replies without hesitation that man should not consider his material possessions as his own, but as common to all . . .", because "above the laws and judgments of men stands the law, the judgment of Christ" (CA 30).

Jesus does not teach that the rich cannot be saved. He teaches that it will not be easy. Giving up material ownership for the sake of the kingdom—the way to perfection—is the better thing. All followers of Jesus, each of us, should own property as if it were on loan from God. After all, he has entrusted property to us. "The Lord's are the earth and its fullness, the world and those who dwell in it" (Ps 24).

The Second Vatican Council teaches:

In his use of things man should regard the external goods he legitimately owns not merely as exclusive to himself but common to others also, in the sense they can benefit others as well as himself. Therefore every man has the right to possess a sufficient amount of the earth's goods for himself and his family. (GS 69)

"Whoever has two cloaks should share with the person who has none. And whoever has food should

do likewise" (Lk 3:11). "St. John Chrysostom vigorous-
ly recalls this: 'Not to enable the poor to share in our
goods is to steal from them and deprive them of life.
The goods we possess are not ours, but theirs'" (CCC
2446).

Undue or illicit attachment to material goods can
even lead to the loss of the kingdom of heaven. This
is the teaching of Jesus, his teaching about property
as theft, and how our enslavement to property undercuts our dignity as human persons and imperils our
salvation.

Our own self-worth should never be defined by our
net worth. It is often said that we are what we own.
Jesus' response is that we are what we do with what we
own. Above all, it is a matter of how we help the poor,
for the Lord looks tenderly on those who are poor. He
blesses those who come to the aid of the poor. Love for
the poor is even a motive for the duty to work in order
to have something to share with the poor and needy.

As he does with the other commandments, Jesus
deepens our understanding of the seventh commandment by highlighting a more positive way of respect-
ing property—to see the duty to care for those in need
of property and to come to a healthy detachment from
our own property. "It commands justice and charity in
the care of earthly goods and the fruits of men's labor"
(CCC 2401).

Some Practical and Pastoral Implications

Theft of all kinds is common today, and so often it
is greed that fuels theft. As we see almost daily in the
newspapers, greed is a very hard emotion to keep in

check. Uncertain economic times, to a great extent, have been fueled by greed.

On a more personal level, we experience many kinds of theft today: from neighborhood break-ins to the white-collar crimes, from credit-card fraud to identity theft. All of these inventive ways of theft violate the seventh commandment.

Alfred McBride argues that, on a positive note, the seventh commandment celebrates the value of trust: "Safe homes and neighborhoods arise from trust. A just society originates when the poor trust that they can achieve a decent way of life." There seems to be a great need to encourage and teach the value of trust in our society.

William Barclay writes quite practically of three areas of theft other than the theft of material things where trust is violated and the seventh commandment is often broken in our lives. They include theft of time, theft of innocence, and theft of a person's character and good name. Theft of time includes starting late for work, leaving early, wasting time during the workday, padding one's time sheets. Theft of innocence is based on the admonition of Jesus: "Whoever causes one of these little ones who believe in me to sin, it would be better for him to have a great millstone hung around his neck and to be drowned in the depths of the sea" (Mt 18:6). A person's character and good name are often robbed by gossip in lunchrooms at work, while waiting to pick up children in the parking lot, and by the inappropriate use of Facebook and all kinds of social networks. Such theft is almost impossible to undo.

Both the *Catechism of the Catholic Church* and the *United States Catholic Catechism for Adults* write about the seventh commandment in the context of the larger social teaching of the Church—that "rich treasure of wisdom about building a just society and living lives of holiness amidst the challenges of a modern society" (*USCCA* 421). It is a body of Catholic teaching of which we can be justly proud.

In the section on the seventh commandment, the *United States Catholic Catechism for Adults* sets forth seven major and interrelated themes on Catholic social teaching (*USCCA* 423–24). Briefly, and as a conclusion to this chapter, I list them as follows:

1. Life and Dignity of the Human Person

The dignity of the human person, and its protection, is foundational to our moral vision for society. This value is increasingly undercut in contemporary society. Abortion, abuse of the death penalty, use of embryonic stem cells in research, and assisted suicide are the most obvious areas of violation in our day.

2. Call to Family, Community, and Participation

This underscores the "social" nature of a person. Often under attack, the central social institution of the family is worth preserving and strengthening. The family has traditionally been called the "domestic church."

3. Rights and Responsibilities

Each person has a fundamental right to life and what is required for a decent human life. Along with these rights are the duties and responsibilities toward each other, our families, and the greater society.

4. Option for the Poor and Vulnerable

The needs of the poor and vulnerable must be put first. The story of the Last Judgment (Mt 25:31–46) reminds us that we will be judged depending on how we treat the least among us. The Catholic Church has demonstrated over and over again its incredible support for the poor and vulnerable throughout the world. There is a preferential option for the poor. What an incredible witness to the credibility of our faith!

5. The Dignity of Work and the Rights of Workers

Work makes us co-creators with God. The Church has always been on the side of workers, arguing for their right to productive work, decent and fair wages, and the right to organize and join unions.

6. Solidarity

Increasingly, we are challenged to understand the global and international consequences of our domestic economy with all the global and interdependent challenges and opportunities that it produces. We are one human family.

7. Care for the Environment

The respect for our Creator is concretely demonstrated by our stewardship of creation. The environmental challenge has moral and ethical dimensions that cannot be ignored by any one of us. "Care for the earth is a requirement of our faith" (USCCA 424).

These seven themes are starting points to help us see the proscription against theft in its broader social context.

The challenge to trust exists for each of us. The grace is available from God. Now must come our joyful response of faith. Quite simply: don't steal. Act with justice and love.

Reflect

1. If you have been the victim of a theft of some kind, how did it affect you?

2. What have you done or can you do to help restore trust in your family, neighborhood, and wider society?

3. How do you integrate Christ's call to live justly into . . .

    your personal life?

    your family life?

    your professional life?

Pray

Almighty and eternal God.
May your grace enkindle in all of us
a love for the many unfortunate people
whom poverty and misery
reduce to a condition of life
unworthy of human beings.

Arouse in the hearts of those who call you
    Father
a hunger and thirst for social justice
and for fraternal charity
in deeds and in truth.

Grant, O Lord,
peace in our days,
peace to souls,
peace to families,
peace to our country,
and peace among nations.

—Pius XII

EIGHT

The Eighth Commandment: The Truth Will Set You Free

The concepts of freedom and truth are as American as apple pie. We speak of "Honest Abe." We quote Mark Twain, who once was reported to have said: "When in doubt, tell the truth." In court, one swears "to tell the truth, the whole truth, and nothing but the truth." Truth is at the heart of the adversarial system in the courtroom, where the entire purpose of all the procedural safeguards is to get at the truth.

Words are not the only medium of truth. As Catholics, we have a special devotion to St. Joseph, the foster father of Jesus. The late Holy Father John Paul II writes of St. Joseph: "The Gospels do not record any word ever spoken by Joseph. . . . But the silence of Joseph has its own special eloquence, for thanks to that silence we can understand the truth of the Gospel's judgment that he was 'a just man' (Mt 1:19)" (CR 17). Even in silence, there is a truth. Witness is a form of truth, and sometimes witness radiates the credibility of a freeing truth more than words themselves.

The eighth commandment is "You shall not bear false witness against your neighbor"(Ex 20:16; Dt 5:20). Remembering the words of Jesus, "The truth will set you free," we continue with our three-fold method: analysis of the Jewish understanding of the commandment, the

106

effect of the Christ event on the commandment, and some practical and pastoral implications.

The Jewish Understanding of the Commandment

Relying on the very first book of the Old Testament, Alfred McBride writes:

> Scripture is quite clear about the evil of lying. The very first sin recorded in the Bible, the disobedience of Adam and Eve, was occasioned by the serpent's lie: "You certainly will not die! No, God knows well that the moment you eat of it your eyes will be opened and you will be like gods . . ." (Gn 3:4b–5a). From that moment on, the devil, personified in the garden by the serpent, is called the "father of lies" (cf. Jn 8:44).

At its heart, however, in the Jewish mentality, the eighth commandment was originally a forensic commandment or one related to legal proceedings or debate. Its setting was the courtroom. It was a commandment whose purpose was directed primarily toward guarding the basic right of the covenant member against the threat of a false accusation. It dealt with the obligation of a witness in a court of law. "The truth, the whole truth, and nothing but the truth" was required of every witness under the Jewish legal system. In fact, the Jewish law took great pains to ensure that such legal testimony was reliable and true. The Hebrew word for truth, *emeth*, "refers both to truth in words and truthfulness in deeds" (*USCCA* 431).

Regarding the number of witnesses and the fate of a false witness, the book of Deuteronomy is quite clear:

> One witness alone shall not take the stand against a man in regard to any crime or any offense of which he may be guilty; a judicial fact shall be established only on the testimony of two or three witnesses. If an unjust witness takes the stand against a man to accuse him of a defection from the law, the two parties in the dispute shall appear before the LORD in the presence of the priests or judges in office at that time; and if after a thorough investigation the judges find that the witness is a false witness and has accused his kinsman falsely, you shall do to him as he planned to do to his kinsman. Thus shall you purge the evil from your midst. The rest, on hearing of it, shall fear, and never again do a thing so evil among you. Do not look on such a man with pity. Life for life, eye for eye, tooth for tooth, hand for hand, and foot for foot. (Dt 19:15–21)

The Jewish trial procedure depended heavily upon the testimony of witnesses and made little use of physical evidence. The concurring testimony of two witnesses was sufficient to convict a person of a crime. The rule invited abuse, however, by those who stood to gain from another's injury. Hence there was the need for this protective commandment in the covenant community. There were widespread abuses, nevertheless.

The story of Susanna, who was accused of adultery, is a classic example of such abuse. Two witnesses were found to have testified falsely against her.

> The whole assembly cried aloud, blessing God who saves those that hope in him. They rose up against the two elders, for by their own words Daniel had convicted them of perjury. According to the law of Moses, they inflicted on them the penalty they had plotted to impose on their neighbor: they put them to death. Thus was innocent blood spared that day. (Dn 13:60–62)

"'Your fine lie has cost you also your head,' said Daniel; 'for the angel of God waits with a sword to cut you in two so as to make an end of you both'" (Dn 13:59).

A more familiar example is found in 1 Kings 21. It is the story of the trial of Naboth, a vivid example of the violent possibilities when a court is perverted by lying witnesses. The story involves Ahab, the king of Israel; his Phoenician wife Jezebel; and a man named Naboth. When Naboth refuses Ahab's offer to purchase his vineyard, Jezebel arranges to have false charges brought against Naboth, accusing him of cursing both God and king. As punishment, Naboth is stoned to death, and Ahab takes possession of Naboth's vineyard—a clear violation of the eighth commandment against bearing false witnesses against a neighbor.

Moreover, the Wisdom literature from the Psalms and Proverbs is replete with examples of the condemnation of false and malicious witnesses. One of the six things the Lord hates is "the false witness who utters lies" (Prv 6:19). For the Psalmist, he perceives that "malicious and lying witnesses have risen against me" (Ps 27:12). "Lying lips are an abomination to the Lord, but those who are truthful are his delight" (Prv 12:22). In Sirach we read: "A liar's way leads to dishonor, his shame remains ever with him" (Sir 20:25).

Above all, it was in the legal proceeding where truth or falsehood was determined. It was, for the Israelites, the place from which the blessing of truth and corruption of falsehood originated and from which it spread to the people and to their neighbors. It shows how important the Israelite's neighbor was to him in the question of truth—a neighbor was one with full citizenship in the covenant community. It is tempting to speak of the eighth commandment as having a paradigmatic character, i.e., one who is truthful in court would be truthful in other spheres of life.

But there is a deeper religious basis to the eighth commandment—a basis that links it, as with all the commandments, to the covenant itself. Integrity and honesty, after all, were required in the covenant community. To lie or bring false charges violated faithfulness to God and neighbor and was thus a violation of the eighth commandment. Daily life would be negatively affected where transparency and honesty in personal relationships were jeopardized, even and particularly apart from legal proceedings.

Serious and destructive perversions of the truth would thus damage the life of the community and would undercut how free people should be living together in harmony and honesty.

Hence, the eighth commandment as it developed over time, and as it came to be understood by the Jewish mentality, included a more general injunction against lying and on behalf of truth telling. The Old Testament does indeed expand the force of this commandment by connecting the witness in the court with the more general practices of lying and particularly of slander.

The Effect of the Christ Event on the Commandment

"In Jesus Christ, the whole of God's truth has been made manifest" (*CCC* 2466). The word *truth*, the underlying value of the eighth commandment, is another name for Jesus himself. Truth becomes personalized in him, in his very person. Jesus teaches after all: "I am the way and the truth and the life, no one comes to the Father except through me" (Jn 14:6). We read further in the First Letter of John: "Whoever says, 'I know him,' but does not keep his commandments is a liar" (1 Jn 2:4).

In the Sermon on the Mount, where he repeatedly stretched, radicalized, and internalized aspects of the Mosaic law, Jesus clearly indicates his unconditional love for the truth. In Matthew he states: "Let your 'Yes' mean 'Yes,' and your 'No' mean 'No'" (Mt 5:37). In John, when he describes the evil one, he refers to truth as well. Jesus says: "He was a murderer from the beginning and does not stand in truth, because there is no truth in him. When he tells a lie, he speaks in character, because he is a liar and the father of lies" (Jn 8:44). In Colossians, St. Paul discourages lying: "Stop lying to one another" (Col 3:9). In Ephesians, the same Paul exhorts the early Christian community, and us as well, to "speak the truth, each one to his neighbor, for we are members one of another" (Eph 4:25).

About himself, Jesus says: "I am . . . the truth" (Jn 14:16). Note the contrast then—the evil one is the father of lies and Jesus is the truth. Jesus not only is in possession of the truth; Jesus personifies the truth. He personalizes the eighth commandment. In his very person, he is the truth.

But what does this mean? Much can be said about the meaning of truth. Historical truth means that something really happened in reality, in a certain way, at a certain time in history. Philosophical truth means the highest reality, the truth of the Supreme Being. But in John 14, when Jesus says he is the truth; or when in John 18 in his dialogue with Pilate, who asks rhetorically, "What is truth?" Jesus says—speaking of truth: "For this I was born, and for this I came into the world, to testify to the truth. Everyone who belongs to the truth listens to my voice" (Jn 18:37–38).

But what does this truth mean—this truth with which Jesus identifies his very person and mission? Simply stated, it is the revealing, the unpacking, the manifestation of God's plan in Jesus. Truth, in this context, is the divine secret revealed. It is the revelation of the mystery of salvation in Jesus Christ, God's unconditional love for us, and our possibility of becoming children of God forever, to share in his divine life—all made possible by the life, death, resurrection of Jesus, and the sending of the Holy Spirit.

It is this truth, the life that Jesus is and brings to us, that sets us free, makes us different kinds of people. Because we live daily with the consequences of original sin, we fall, we doubt, we have our fears. The truth we share in Jesus, i.e., his very life, enables us to live in hope and to live differently. In his historic visit to

Washington in 2008, Benedict XVI reiterated a line from his encyclical on hope: "The one who has hope lives differently; the one who hopes has been granted the gift of a new life" (*SS* 2).

Jesus tells us the truth, his truth. That truth "will set you free" (Jn 8:32), free from sin, from fear, ultimately from death. It is the distinct benefit of belonging to Christ who is the truth. This is the distinct benefit of being baptized into Christ and being literally plunged into the life of God. It is Easter life. What are the implications of this new way of life?

In St. Paul's Letter to the Ephesians, we read language referring to the baptismal liturgy:

> You should put away the old self of your former way of life, corrupted through deceitful desires . . . and put on the new self, created in God's way in righteousness and holiness of truth. Therefore, putting away falsehood, speak the truth, each one to his neighbor, for we are members one of another. (Eph 4:22, 24–25)

Speaking the truth was thus linked to the new life in Christ, a life shared with others, the living body of Christ. Alfred McBride writes:

> Paul considered this baptismal experience motivation to live an honest and truthful moral life, since the candidates belonged to humanity renewed in Christ. Behaving in an honest way towards one's sisters and brothers in Christ was a sign that Christians appreciated what their new existence

demanded. To lie was to act unfaithfully to a member of Christ's body.

There are further implications to this new way of life and the freedom we experience in Christ. Truthful living requires a lifetime of struggle and moral courage. It does not come easily. It takes time and patience. But it does make possible an experience of inner freedom. Such freedom truly does make us free.

This truth, the truth about Jesus, is also a challenge for us who are members of his living body, the Church. It is the challenge to bear witness to the new life that we share, his life. Such witness may call for a great deal, even one's earthly existence, as we have seen from the many martyrs of the last century. "Martyrdom is the supreme witness given to the truth of the faith: it means bearing witness even unto death. The martyr bears witness to Christ who died and rose, to whom he is united by charity" (CCC 2473).

Yes, it means living as Jesus did. His life continues to have something to do with us. After all, he accepted suffering and death as part of the price of living the truth. After his example, we too must give of ourselves. Only in giving of ourselves in love, as he did and does, do we discover our true selves and the truth about our human condition. Only then can we enjoy that deep inner freedom that each of us seeks.

His teaching, as challenging as it can be, really helps us to live differently, to act differently—and to do so with hope, confidence, and joy. This is all born of and, in fact, made possible by the Holy Spirit living within us. "If you remain in my word, you will truly be my disciples, and you will know the truth, and the truth will set you free" (Jn 8:31–32).

Some Practical and Pastoral Implications

The *United States Catholic Catechism for Adults* speaks of the challenge to tell the truth in our present cultural climate.

> In our culture, relativism challenges our ability to tell the truth because it claims there is no objective truth. This attitude undermines the distinction between truth and lies; it leads to an environment of deceit. In such an atmosphere, even Christ's teachings, based on divine truth, fail to persuade those whose trust in the possibility of objective truth has disappeared. This is the climate in which the Church needs to call people back to the reality of objective truth and to the link between doctrinal truth and everyday life." (*USCCA* 431)

Implications of this analysis can be found in the op-ed pages of our newspapers. The Catechism teaches that "the more our culture has moved away from acceptance of objective truth, the more it has moved toward the culture of opinions" (*USCCA* 435). The culture of opinions has become effectively a national pastime. In this culture, everyone is entitled to his or her opinion, and such opinion can take on a certain seeming credibility.

Where then can we find objective truth, truth revealed by truth himself, other than Christ and his living body, the Church? So often in our day it is hard to see that truth, the truth about the marriage between a man and a woman, the truth about the openness to new life, the truth about the protection of all life—from a tiny baby in the womb, to a deadly criminal whose fate might too easily be the death chamber, to an elderly person whose dignity might easily be overlooked and thus discarded. The truth sets us free, and it challenges us to see truth and witness to the truth in our culture.

The Catechism gives us examples of individuals who valued truth so much that they were willing to die for it. Two such individuals, St. John Fisher and St. Thomas More, "surrendered their lives rather than approve of the divorce of King Henry VIII or deny the truth that the pope is Christ's appointed head of the Church" (*USCCA* 432). In effect, they died rather than go against their properly formed conscience, a conscience formed in them by Christ's own truth. This challenge to conscience increasingly presents a challenge for each of us in our day and will continue to present challenges for us in the days and years to come. Are we prepared to stand up for the truth, the only truth that truly sets us free?

On a more practical level, the Catechism teaches: "Lying consists in saying what is false with the intention of deceiving one's neighbor" (*CCC* 2508). Our society is replete with a culture of dishonesty—between parents and children, in courts, in the workplace, and even between doctors and lawyers and their patients and clients. Is it then even possible to live the eighth commandment in a culture that is so skeptical of the possibility of knowing the truth? I would emphatically assert that it is.

Such a life is found in Christ. It is a life of living his commandments, a life of repenting often of our sinfulness, a life of appropriating daily the life-giving teachings of our faith. It is, above all, a faith in the very person of Jesus, who describes himself as the way, the truth, and the life. Only such a life makes truth-telling possible and even appealing. This is true even in our culture of relativism and skepticism. But it takes more conscious efforts daily to live a life of truth.

St. Augustine puts it succinctly and comprehensively: "When regard for truth has been broken down or even slightly weakened, all things remain doubtful." In contrast, the truth—i.e., life in Christ—will set us free. Of this, there is no doubt.

Reflect

1. What are some of the consequences of lying or withholding truth that you have observed personally or professionally?

2. How does one know when to keep silent or when to speak out about a significant matter?

Pray

Jesus, Prince of all Heavenly Truths,
your words are carved for eternity!
You have commanded the virtue of honesty,
it is the power against all deceptions.
Direct your spirit of honesty upon me,
that my soul may always remain stainless.
Guide my daily thoughts, words, and
    actions,

to join those living by the spirit of truth.
For honesty yields harmony and loyalty,
enriching all human relationships.
By the power of your Spirit that flourishes,
honesty will prevail in this world!

—Catholic Doors Ministry

NINE

The Ninth and Tenth
Commandments:
Purity and Poverty of Heart

In this final chapter, both the ninth and tenth commandments are treated together. In the Catholic
tradition, they share in common the word *covet*.
The ninth commandment states: "You shall not covet
your neighbor's wife," and the tenth commandment
states: "You shall not covet your neighbor's goods."
These commandments need not be viewed simply in a
negative way—a proscription against coveting. There
is another way to look at them that emphasizes their
positive dimension. In light of the Beatitudes, we may
see them, as the title of this chapter suggests, as a call to
purity and poverty of heart.

The Jewish
Understanding of These Two Commandments

In Exodus, the second book of the Bible, the word
covet is used twice. It applies both to coveting another's
wife and goods. "You shall not covet your neighbor's
house. You shall not covet your neighbor's wife, nor
his male or female slave, nor his ox or ass, nor anything
else that belongs to him" (Ex 20:17). The word *covet* is

used there first with respect to a neighbor's house as an object and second with respect to a neighbor's wife. In Deuteronomy, by way of contrast, the word *covet* is used only once and with respect to a neighbor's wife as object. In the second part of Deuteronomy's version of this commandment, *desire* is used, and its object is the neighbor's house and belongings. "You shall not covet your neighbor's wife. You shall not desire your neighbor's house or field, nor his male or female slave, nor his ox or ass, nor anything that belongs to him" (Dt 5:20).

Among biblical scholars, there has been much discussion regarding the meaning of the word *covet*. In a nutshell, the question is whether the Hebrew word for *covet* means simply an emotion, an inordinate desire for something not one's own, the disposition of an individual in the direction of the deed; or whether it also includes the action that stems from the emotion. In the Hebrew language and culture, the distinction between cause and effect is often blurred. Often the desire and the resulting action are seen as a deep unity. The best synthesis—taking into account that the Exodus word for *covet* is *hamad* and the Deuteronomic word is *hit'awweh*—is that, for the Jewish mind, desiring and the resultant deed are closely related. But they are not identical and not necessarily simultaneous acts. The emphasis in the word *hamad* falls on the emotion (desire) which often leads to a commensurate action; whereas the focus of *hit'awweh* rests only on the emotion itself, the very strong desire, indeed the craving for something not one's own.

The Jewish understanding of *covet* thus does not necessarily imply active misappropriation. The mere fact that the verb *hamad* occasionally implies some act of seizure or the like does not entail that such an act must always belong to its proper meaning. Fundamentally, what is proscribed is thus a guard against an internal attitude or feeling that tends to erupt into public and violent acts against one's neighbor.

Consider again King Ahab's coveting Naboth's vineyard, his desire to have the adjoining property as his vegetable garden. This is an excellent example of how an inordinate inner feeling of envy or greed can lead to an act that can be in violation of the tenth commandment. Such feelings are at the heart of the Jewish understanding of the proscription against covetousness. Such inner feelings of envious and greedy desire—left unchecked—can lead to the violation of any and all the commandments against killing, adultery, stealing, and bearing false witness. This is precisely what happens in the story of Ahab's coveting Naboth's vineyard in 1 Kings 21:1–29. When Naboth refuses to give him the property, subsequent acts of false witness, judicial murder, and royal theft take place. These acts did not find favor with God.

Focus once more on the story of King David's passion for Bathsheba that we examined in reviewing the sixth commandment. Although she is a married woman, Bathsheba is seduced by David. Dealing with the underlying issue here, Alfred McBride writes:

> In his psalm of repentance, David does not talk about adultery or murder. He does not list his woeful behaviors. He talks about his heart because he knows that is where the real trouble lies. He knows perfectly well that adultery and murder are terrible acts, but he realizes it is far more important to

get at the heart of the matter: "A clean heart
create for me, God; and a steadfast spirit
renew with me. Cast me not out from your
presence . . . give me back the joy of your
salvation . . ." (Ps 51:12–13a,14a). Behavior
modification, useful as it may be, would not
solve David's problem. He digs deeper and
asks for a conversion of heart. He believes
that God can make this happen, so he pleads
for the creation of a clean heart. His new
heart will bring him three things: a steadfast
spirit, a constant union of love with God and
joy of salvation.

It was David's lust that led ultimately to the act
of adultery—his coveting another man's wife; and, as
with King Ahab in the previous example, it is that inner
desire that violates the biblical law against coveting.

The Effect of the
Christ Event on These Commandments

The proscription against coveting in the Old Testament forms a bridge to the ninth and tenth commandments as understood by Jesus. Patrick Miller writes that
this proscription

> . . . creates a bridge or inaugurates a trajectory
> leading directly to Jesus' internalization of the
> commandments in the Sermon on the Mount
> (Mt 5:21–30). The observation that feelings
> of anger and lust cannot be controlled in the
> same way in which murder and adultery can
> be controlled is to an extent true, but as a

sole response to Jesus' injunctions against those emotions this is inadequate. Already in the commandment against coveting the clear connection between internal feelings and external acts, between private attitudes and public deeds, is explicitly recognized. The point is clear. The inner attitudes and feelings have to do potentially with the well-being and security of one's neighbor, and they are subject to a degree of control for the good of the community. Jesus' teaching, therefore, like that of the rabbis and philosophers, is an extension of the instruction clearly set forth in the last commandment [against coveting] and illustrated negatively so often in the Scriptures and in human life.

When we read the ninth commandment against coveting a neighbor's wife, how can we not think of Jesus' proscription in the Sermon on the Mount against lust in the heart? He taught that everyone who looks at a woman with lust has already committed adultery. In that one line, Jesus links lustful feelings with a prohibited action.

But lust, the principal object of the ninth commandment, must be seen in a broader context. "St. Paul identifies it with the rebellion of the 'flesh' against the 'spirit'" (CCC 2515). In Romans, he teaches: "If you live according to the flesh, you will die, but if by the spirit you put to death the deeds of the body, you will live" (Rom 8:13). Now this flesh, according to Paul, is not the skin on our hand or on our body. For Paul, it is that internal powerful drive within each of us toward self-preservation, self-glorification, and selfishness. It is a bondage to sin that causes us to resist God and to be alienated from him. It is a product of the disobedience of the first sin of Adam. Lust, for example, proceeds from the flesh. Except for Christ's death, resurrection and sending of the Holy Spirit, each of us would continue to live at the level of the flesh. "All of us once lived among them in the desires of our flesh, following the wishes of the flesh and the impulses. . . . But God, who is rich in mercy . . . brought us to life with Christ" (Eph 2:3–5).

This does not mean we are without struggles, the struggles of the flesh, the struggles of covetousness. There is spiritual warfare within each of us. It is an integral part of the truth of the human person. In Galatians, St. Paul is explicit about the battle between the flesh and spirit (cf. Gal 5:16–26). In the *Confessions of St. Augustine*, we read:

> The enemy had taken hold of my will; he had clamped a chain on it and shackled it. For my will had been perverted and had manufactured lust; the more I gave in to lust, the more it developed into a habit, and when I failed to check the habit it became a necessity. These were all links in the chain that held me enslaved. The new will that had begun in me—and made me want to be free to worship and to enjoy you, God, the only certain joy—was not yet strong enough to overpower the old will that had become tough with age. So there were now two wills battling it out inside me, one old, one new; one carnal, one spiritual; and in the conflict they ripped my soul to pieces.

The call of the ninth commandment, precisely because of the Christ event, is to crucify our flesh, our passions, our lust, and our inordinate desires. In effect, it requires daily surrender to the power of the Holy Spirit living within us, and yielding to the movement of the Spirit so that our flesh might be crucified. "Now those who belong to Christ Jesus have crucified their flesh with its passions and desires. If we live in the Spirit, let us also follow the Spirit" (Gal 5:24–25).

We need to take personal responsibility for our sins, the sins of our flesh, and make a specific decision to die to them. Through the grace of Baptism, the Holy Spirit makes that decision active within us when we are joined to the death and resurrection of Jesus. It happens, moreover, each and every time we repent in the sacrament of Penance. Hence, repentance underscores the integral importance of that sacrament in the struggle with our flesh, the covetousness proscribed by the ninth commandment. And what a reward awaits us: "Blessed are the clean of heart, for they shall see God" (Mt 5:8).

We turn now to the tenth commandment, the proscription against greed: "You shall not covet your neighbor's goods." Jesus could not be more explicit with respect to this commandment: "Take care to guard against all greed, for though one may be rich, one's life does not consist of possessions" (Lk 12:15). He even goes so far as to say: "Everyone of you who does not renounce all his possessions cannot be my disciple" (Lk 14:33). Pointing to the case of the widow's mite, he holds her up as a wonderful example of Christian living: "I tell you truly, this poor widow put in more than all the rest; for those others have all made offerings from their surplus wealth, but she, from her poverty, has offered her whole livelihood" (Lk 21:3–4).

Greed is thus clearly proscribed by Christ. Importantly, however, generosity, even from our poverty, is required if we are to be his followers. It goes hand in hand with a sense of detachment from worldly goods. Both are essential values underlying the tenth commandment.

He teaches, after all, in the Sermon on the Mount: "Blessed are the poor in spirit" (Mt 5:3). A certain detachment from riches is thus the continuing goal of life in Christ, that we might follow him all the more closely and without competition from earthly material temptations. "If then you were raised with Christ, seek what is above. . . . Think of what is above, not of what is on earth" (Col 3:1–2). Jesus teaches us to rely on him and him alone: "Therefore I tell you, do not worry about your life and what you will eat, or about your body and what you will wear. For life is more than food and the body more than clothing" (Lk 12:22–23). St. Paul is quite explicit in Ephesians where he writes: "Be sure of this, that no immoral or impure or greedy person, that is, an idolater, has any inheritance in the kingdom of Christ and of God" (Eph 5:5). For Jesus, covetousness is thus a form of idolatry. "Where your treasure is, there also will be your heart" (Mt 6:21).

Some Practical and Pastoral Implications

With respect to the ninth commandment, the underlying values are chastity, purity of heart, and self-control. We hear the perennial question of the psalmist in Psalm 24: "Who may go up the mountain of the LORD? Who can stand in his holy place?" And the answer: "The clean of hand and pure of heart." Oh, how we so desire to climb his mountain and stand with him in his holy place! It is within our reach, with God's help and grace. Our goal is a pure heart, and yet, as the Catechism acknowledges, there is a struggle, a battle for purity within each and every one of us. It is good to admit to that and not to live in a wonderland of deception.

But the battle can be won each and every day. Alfred McBride writes:

> Sex is a strong passion, but not a blind instinct. Humans can control it. Despite many teachings to the contrary, self-control is the road to real freedom, while free love abandons self-control and makes sex the slave of passion. Sexual license is clearly the opposite of freedom. Chaste living implies control of thoughts and desires as well as behavior. Jesus was quite direct on this issue: "But I say to you, everyone who looks at a woman with lust has already committed adultery with her in his heart" (Mt 5:28). A chaste person practices modesty and lives a lifestyle that reflects a commitment to purity.

The talk of chastity today is, for sure, counter-cultural if not downright unfashionable and politically incorrect. But for us Christians, chastity is part of the newfound freedom we enjoy by virtue of Christ's resurrection and the sending of the Holy Spirit. Each of our bodies is a part of the risen body of Christ. Our bodies are holy places precisely because we are an integral part of his glorified body. To sin in mind or deed sexually with our bodies, bodies linked to Christ at Baptism, is to make sacrilegious use of Christ's body, to which we belong.

In the 1990 document of the American bishops entitled *Human Sexuality*, the bishops define chastity in this way:

> Chastity "consists in self-control, in the capacity of guiding the sexual instinct to the service of love and of integrating it in the development of the person." Chastity is often misunderstood as simply a suppression or deliberate inhibition of sexual thoughts, feelings, and actions. However, chastity truly consists in the long-term integration of one's thoughts, feelings and actions in a way that values, esteems, and respects the dignity of oneself and others. Chastity frees us from the tendency to act in a manipulative or exploitative manner in our relationships and enables us to show true love and kindness always.

To win the battle for chastity, one must be eminently practical. If the computer is the problem, one must be smart in protecting oneself against its use for impurity. If certain friendships are the problem, there are ways diplomatically to move in other circles. If modesty is the challenge, there are other ways to dress and behave, and each of us knows the difference.

Most practically, there is the regular reception of the sacrament of Reconciliation, daily prayer, and the commitment to make of chastity an integral part of our desire to follow Christ unreservedly. And, of course, in addition to the grace of Christ, there are prayers direct-ed to our Blessed Mother that she might accompany us on our daily journey to live a chaste life. The life of chastity is assuredly both challenging and rewarding.

As we focus on the tenth commandment, we learn that we should avoid greed, envy, and the pre-occupation with money and material possessions. We live in a world of insatiable appetites for food, plea-sure, luxuries, and all kinds of gadgets. Especially in times of economic uncertainty, these appetites present new opportunities for us to re-examine our values and goals. To what extent does peer pressure determine our life style? How often are the choices of our neighbors uncritically accepted and seen as a recipe for automatic happiness? It is, above all, this belief that covetousness of things can bring us happiness. It is a lesson that we need to learn: that it is not things, but the person of Christ himself, who should be our preoccupation in life. Covetousness is thus a form of idolatry—things replac-ing the person of Jesus Christ.

St. Paul is so clear when he writes: "For the love of money is the root of all evils, and some people in their desire for it have strayed from the faith and have pierced themselves with many pains" (1 Tm 6:10). Love of money, however, is different than a healthy respect for money. And there is no better way to learn respect for money than by the virtue of generosity. At the base of the tenth commandment is the challenge to be gener-ous—to pursue and develop a generous heart.

So many people are deeply generous. Being gener-ous is the best antidote to greed and all that the tenth commandment seeks to prevent. Generous people are everywhere. They help in hospitals, shelters, parish programs, pro-bono legal and medical networks, annual toy collections, monthly food drives, and tutoring in schools. Generosity is also evidenced by contributions to diocesan and parish collections as well as to the poor box.

William Barclay, whom I have cited previously in this book, sets forth five guidelines for giving, which the Jewish rabbis in biblical times laid down. They are as helpful for us today as they were for them in ancient times. The guidelines are:

1. Giving must not be refused.

2. Giving must befit the man to whom the gift is given.

3. Giving must be carried out privately and secretly.

4. The manner of giving must befit the character and the temperament of the recipient.

5. Giving is at once a privilege and an obligation, for in reality all giving is nothing less than giving to God.

There is no better way to fight the innate temptation for greed than through generosity of spirit. As the Catechism teaches, "Detachment from riches is necessary for entering the kingdom of heaven. 'Blessed are the poor in spirit'" (CCC 2556).

Reflect

1. How would you define the word *covet*?

2. What is the opposite of greed? Of lust?

3. What are some ways to deal with wrongful desires?

4, How would you describe your heart's desire?

Pray

Do not be provoked by evildoers;
do not envy those who do wrong.
Like grass they wither quickly;
like green plants they wilt away.
Trust in the Lord and do good
that you may dwell in the land and live
   secure.
Find your delight in the Lord
who will give you your heart's desire.
Commit your way to the Lord;
trust that God will act
and make your integrity shine like the
   dawn,
your vindication like noonday.
Be still before the Lord; wait for God.
Do not be provoked by the prosperous,
nor by malicious schemers.

—Psalm 37

Appendix

A Guide to Confession and an Examination of Conscience

This guide is reproduced by permission of the Archdiocese of Washington. It was created as a part of "The Light Is ON for You" program and can be found online at www.adw.org/parishes/ tlio/guide.html

The Sacrament of Penance, or Confession, brings about a change of heart through God's mercy and forgiveness. Experience the Lord's compassion through the Sacrament of Penance, which is made up of the following parts: Before, During, and After.

Before

How to Make a Good Confession

Confession is not difficult, but it does require preparation. We should begin with prayer, placing ourselves in the presence of God, our loving Father. We seek healing and forgiveness through repentance and a resolve to sin no more. Then we review our lives since our last confession, searching our thoughts, words, and actions for that which did not conform to God's command to love him and one another through his laws and the laws of his Church. This is called an examination of conscience.

To make an examination of conscience:

- Begin with a prayer asking for God's help.
- Review your life with the help of some questions, which are based on the Ten Commandments (see below).
- Tell God how truly sorry you are for your sins.
- Make a firm resolution not to sin again.

Examination of Conscience

Recall your sins. Prayerfully ask yourself what you have done with full knowledge and full consent against God's and the Church's commandments.

1. I am the Lord your God. You shall not have strange gods before Me.

   - Do I give God time every day in prayer?
   - Do I seek to love Him with my whole heart?
   - Have I been involved with superstitious practices, or have I been involved with the occult?
   - Do I seek to surrender myself to God's Word as taught by the Church?
   - Have I ever received Communion in the state of mortal sin?
   - Have I ever deliberately told a lie in Confession, or have I withheld a mortal sin from the priest in Confession?

2. You shall not take the name of the Lord your God in vain.

- Have I used God's name in vain: lightly or carelessly?
- Have I been angry with God?
- Have I wished evil upon any other person?
- Have I insulted a sacred person or abused a sacred object?

3. Remember to keep holy the Lord's Day.

- Have I deliberately missed Mass on Sundays or Holy Days of Obligation?
- Have I tried to observe Sunday as a family day and a day of rest?
- Do I do needless work on Sunday?

4. Honor your father and your mother.

- Do I honor and obey my parents?
- Have I neglected my duties to my spouse and children?
- Have I given my family good religious example?
- Do I try to bring peace into my home life?
- Do I care for my aged and infirm relatives?

5. You shall not kill.

- Have I had an abortion or encouraged anyone to have an abortion?
- Have I physically harmed anyone?
- Have I abused alcohol or drugs?
- Did I give scandal to anyone, thereby leading him or her into sin?
- Have I been angry or resentful?
- Have I harbored hatred in my heart?
- Have I mutilated myself through any form of sterilization?

- Have I encouraged or condoned sterilization?

6. You shall not commit adultery.

   - Have I been faithful to my marriage vows in thought and action?
   - Have I engaged in any sexual activity outside of marriage?
   - Have I used any method of contraception or artificial birth control?
   - Has each sexual act in my marriage been open to the transmission of new life?
   - Have I been guilty of masturbation?
   - Have I sought to control my thoughts?
   - Have I respected all members of the opposite sex, or have I thought of other people as objects?
   - Have I been guilty of any homosexual activity?
   - Do I seek to be chaste in my thoughts, words and actions?
   - Am I careful to dress modestly?

7. You shall not steal.

   - Have I stolen what is not mine?
   - Have I returned or made restitution for what I have stolen?
   - Do I waste time at work, school, or home?
   - Do I gamble excessively, thereby denying my family of their needs?
   - Do I pay my debts promptly?
   - Do I seek to share what I have with the poor?

8. You shall not bear false witness against your neighbor.

   - Have I lied?
   - Have I gossiped?
   - Have I spoken behind someone else's back?
   - Am I sincere in my dealings with others?
   - Am I critical, negative, or uncharitable in my thoughts of others?
   - Do I keep secret what should be kept confidential?

9. You shall not desire your neighbor's wife.

   - Have I consented to impure thoughts?
   - Have I caused them by impure reading, movies, conversation, or curiosity?
   - Do I seek to control my imagination?
   - Do I pray at once to banish impure thoughts and temptations?

10. You shall not desire your neighbor's goods.

   - Am I jealous of what other people have?
   - Do I envy other people's families or possessions?
   - Am I greedy or selfish?
   - Are material possessions the purpose of my life?
   - Do I trust that God will care for all of my material and spiritual needs?

An examination of conscience for young people, for married couples, and for single people can be found at: www.adw.org/parishes/tlio/guide.html.

During

What is Reconciliation?

Reconciliation (also known as Confession or Penance) is a sacrament instituted by Jesus Christ in His love and mercy to offer sinners forgiveness for offenses committed against God. At the same time, sinners reconcile with the Church because it is also wounded by our sins.

Every time we sin, we hurt ourselves, other people, and God. In Reconciliation, we acknowledge our sins before God and his Church. We express our sorrow in a meaningful way, receive the forgiveness of Christ and his Church, make reparation for what we have done, and resolve to do better in the future.

The forgiveness of sins involves four parts:

- Contrition: a sincere sorrow for having offended God, and the most important act of the penitent. There can be no forgiveness of sin if we do not have sorrow and a firm resolve not to repeat our sin.
- Confession: confronting our sins in a profound way to God by speaking about them—aloud—to the priest.
- Penance: an important part of our healing is the "penance" the priest imposes in reparation for our sins.
- Absolution: the priest speaks the words by which "God, the Father of Mercies" reconciles a sinner to himself through the merits of the Cross.

Rite of Reconciliation

Reconciliation may be face-to-face or anonymous, with a screen between you and the priest. Choose the option that is the most comfortable for you.

The priest gives you a blessing or greeting. He may share a brief Scripture passage.

Make the Sign of the Cross and say: "Bless me father, for I have sinned. My last confession was . . . (give the number of weeks, months, or years).

Confess all of your sins to the priest. The priest will help you to make a good confession. If you are unsure about how to confess or you feel uneasy, just ask him to help you. Answer his questions without hiding anything out of fear or shame. Place your trust in God, a merciful Father who wants to forgive you.

Following your confession of sins, say: "I am sorry for these and all of my sins."

The priest assigns you a penance and offers advice to help you be a better Catholic.

Say an Act of Contrition, expressing your sorrow for your sins. The priest, acting in the person of Christ, then absolves you from your sins.

Act of Contrition

God, I am heartily sorry for having offended you, and I detest all my sins because I dread the loss of heaven and the pains of hell; but most of all because they offend you, my God, who are all good and deserving of all my love. I firmly resolve with the help of your grace to confess my sins, do penance, and to amend my life. Amen.

After

Rejoice! You have received the forgiveness of Christ! What should you do when you leave? Remember the words you recited in the Act of Contrition: "I firmly intend, with your help, to do penance, to sin no more, and to avoid whatever leads me to sin."

Before you leave the confessional, the priest will give you your penance, which may consist of prayer, an offering, works of mercy, or sacrifices. These works help to join us with Christ, who alone died for us. The goal of our life's journey is to grow closer to God. We can do this through prayer, spiritual reading, fasting, and the reception of the sacraments.

Abbreviations

CA On the Hundredth Anniversary of Rerum Novarum (Centesimus Annus). Encyclical of Pope John Paul II, 1991.

CR Guardian of the Redeemer (Custos Redemptoris). Apostolic Exhortation of Pope John Paul II, 1989.

DCE God Is Love (Deus Caritas Est). Encyclical of Pope Benedict XVI, 2006.

DD The Lord's Day (Dies Domini). Apostolic Letter of Pope John Paul II, 1998.

DP The Dignity of a Person (Dignitas Personae). Congregation for the Doctrine of the Faith, 2008.

DV Dogmatic Constitution on Divine Revelation (Dei Verbum). Vatican Council II, 1965.

GS The Church in the Modern World (Gaudium et Spes). Pastoral Constitution of Vatican Council II, 1965.

SC The Sacrament of Charity (Sacramentum Caritatis). Apostolic Exhortation of Pope Benedict XVI, 2007.

SS Saved by Hope (Spe Salvi). Encyclical of Pope Benedict XVI, 2007.

VS On the Splendor of Truth (Veritatis Splendor). Encyclical of Pope John Paul II, 1993.

References

Introduction

Raniero Cantalamessa, *Life in Christ: The Spiritual Message of the Letter to the Romans* (Collegeville, MN: Liturgical Press, 2002), 130.

Austin Flannery, ed., *Vatican Council II: The Conciliar and Post-Conciliar Documents* (Northport, NY: Costello Publishing Company, 1975).

Chapter 1. The One Who Has Faith Lives Differently

Carl A. Anderson, "A Mandate for All Seasons: Catholic Conscience And Secular Society," February 4, 2009, Closing Keynote for the 22nd Workshop for Bishops, Dallas, Texas, 2, 4.

Most Reverend Donald W. Wuerl, "Disciples of the Lord: Sharing the Vision (A Pastoral Letter on the New Evangelization)," August 23, 2010, 4.

Alfred McBride, *The Ten Commandments: Sounds of Love from Sinai* (Cincinnati, OH: St. Anthony Messenger Press, 1990).

Alfred McBride, *The Ten Commandments: Covenant of Love* (Cincinnati, OH: St. Anthony Messenger Press, 2001).

Chapter 2. The First and Second Commandments: Liberating Words of Faith

McBride, 1990, 13.

Chapter 3. The Third Commandment: A Day Set Aside for Love of God

Timothy Dolan, "Keeping the Lord's Day Holy," http://
blog.archny.org/?p=570 (March 17, 2010).

Chapter 4. The Fourth Commandment: Love for Mother and Father—An Unfolding Love

McBride, 2001, 79.

Chapter 5. The Fifth Commandment: Life in Need of Protection

William Barclay, *The Ten Commandments for Today* (New
York: HarperCollins, 1983), 65.

Walter Harrelson, *The Ten Commandments and Human
Rights* (Macon, GA: Mercer University Press, 1997),
115.

McBride, 1990, 69–70.

Chapter 6. The Sixth Commandment: Sex, Marriage, and Purity of Heart

Patrick Miller, *Deuteronomy* (Louisville, KY: J. Knox
Press, 1991), 88–89.

Barclay, 94–95.

David Noel Freedman, "The Nine Commandments,"
Bible Review (December 1989), 36–37.

McBride, 1990, 80.

Carlo Caffarra, *Living in Christ: Fundamental Principles of Catholic Moral Theology* (San Francisco, CA: Ignatius Press, 1987), 219.

Chapter 7. The Seventh Commandment: Don't Steal—Act with Justice and Love

Barclay, 180.

McBride, 1990, 94.

Barclay, 177–79.

Chapter 8. The Eighth Commandment: The Truth Will Set You Free

McBride, 1990, 115.

McBride, 2001, 152.

Chapter 9. The Ninth and Tenth Commandments: Purity and Poverty of Heart

McBride, 2001, 165.

Miller, 96.

Augustine of Hippo, *Love Song: Augustine's Confessions for Modern Man*, trans. Sherwood Eliot Wirt (New York: Harper Row, 1971), 108.

McBride, 2001, 167.

William Barclay, *The Gospel of Matthew, Volume 1* (Louisville, KY: Westminster John Knox Press, 2001), 170–71.

United States Conference of Catholic Bishops, *Human Sexuality: A Catholic Perspective for Education and Life-long Learning* (Washington, DC: USCCB Publishing, 1990), 19.

Monsignor Peter J. Vaghi is pastor of the Church of the Little Flower in Bethesda, Maryland, and a priest of the Archdiocese of Washington. Prior to his seminary studies at the North American College and the Gregorian University in Rome, he practiced law. He remains a member of the Virginia State Bar and the District of Columbia Bar, and is chaplain of the John Carroll Society, a group of professionals and businesspersons in service of the Archbishop of Washington. He is the author of *The Faith We Profess* and *The Sacraments We Celebrate* (Ave Maria Press, 2008, 2010) and has written a number of articles for *America* and *Priest* magazines and for *Our Sunday Visitor* newspaper. He has also contributed to two collections of writings on priestly spirituality: *Behold Your Mother: Priests Speak about Mary* and *Born of the Eucharist: A Spirituality for Priests* (both from Ave Maria Press).